Ginn and Company Ltd

Acknowledgements

Grateful acknowledgement is made to the following for
permission to use copyright material

page 30 **A find for Carlos**
Just a Dog by Helen Griffiths
By kind permission of Hutchinson Publishing Group Limited

54 **Michael at the clinic**
Michael and the Music Makers by Harry Fleming
By kind permission of the publishers, Brockhampton Press
Limited

60 **Sir Henry springs a visit**
Violet for Bonaparte by Geoffrey Trease
By kind permission of Macmillan, London and Basingstoke.

66 **Lucy comes to Hagworthy**
The Wild Hunt of Hagworthy by Penelope Lively
By kind permission of William Heinemann Ltd

78 **Rocky and the lioness**
Rocky and the Lions by R B Maddock
By kind permission of the publishers Thomas Nelson & Sons Ltd

Designed by Michael Soderberg with Alan Miller
Illustrated by Barry Rowe, Martin White and David Atkinson

© Haydn Richards 1965
Revised edition 1981
Eighteenth impression 1993   089307
ISBN 0 602 22548 5 (without answers)
ISBN 0 602 22618 X (with answers)

Published by Ginn and Company Ltd
Prebendal House, Parson's Fee,
Aylesbury, Bucks HP20 2QZ

Filmset by Filmtype Services Limited, Scarborough
Printed in Great Britain at the University Press, Cambridge

Preface

The main aim of Haydn Richards Junior English is to enable the pupil to work alone, as far as is possible. For this reason complete lists of the words needed to answer the various exercises are given. Being thus provided with the necessary tools, the pupil should experience little difficulty in doing the work.

The course provides ample and varied practice in all the English topics usually taught in the Junior School. Such simple grammatical terms as are essential to the understanding of the language are introduced at appropriate stages, together with simple definitions, lucid explanations and easy examples.

The meaning of every proverb and idiom dealt with is given, so that these may be used correctly in both writing and conversation.

A noteworthy feature of each book in the series is the detailed alphabetical Contents, facilitating reference to any particular topic by the teacher and the older pupils.

In addition to teaching and testing such topics as Parts of Speech, Opposites, Synonyms, Homophones, Punctuation, Direct and Indirect Speech, Sentence Linkage and Structure, etc., the course includes verbal intelligence exercises designed to stimulate clear thinking, so that by the end of the fourth year the pupil who has worked steadily through the course is well equipped for any entrance examination.

H.R.

Contents

Nouns

The **postman** found a gold **watch**.

Postman is the **name** of a **person**.

watch is the **name** of a **thing**.

A noun is the name of a person or thing.

A Find the nouns in these sentences.

1 The box was made of wood.

2 The apples were put in a dish.

3 Milk turns sour in hot weather.

4 The lion slept in the shade under the tree.

5 Butter is made from milk.

6 The usherette asked for my ticket.

7 These oranges are used to make marmalade.

8 Did you give the dog his food?

9 In winter the days are short and the nights are long.

10 The children enjoyed their visit to the zoo.

B These are the meanings of ten nouns which are arranged in alphabetical order. Write these nouns.

1 a _ _ _ _ _
the table in the most sacred part of a church

2 b _ _ _ _ _
a hole in the ground made by a rabbit

3 c _ _ _ _ _ _ y
a period of a hundred years

4 d _ _ _ _
the name for a male duck

5 e _ _ _ _
the overhanging edges of a roof

6 f _ _ _ _
a story about animals which can talk

7 g _ _ _ _ _ _
the tallest animal in the world

8 h _ _ _ _ _ _
a tool for beating in nails

9 i _ _ _ _ _ _
land entirely surrounded by water

10 j _ _ _ _ _ _ _
the place where two or more railway lines meet

Verbs

Wilson **trapped** the ball and **scored** a fine goal.

The words **trapped** and **scored** tell **what Wilson did**.

They are doing words, or action words, or verbs.

A verb is a word which shows action.

trickled
sniffed
repaired
wriggled
shuffled
trampled
welcomed
galloped

A Find the verbs in these sentences and write them in your exercise book.

Example 1 washed hung

1 I washed the clothes and hung them on the line.

2 Although he tries hard he makes little progress.

3 Susan folded her sweater and placed it over the back of a chair.

4 When Penny had finished her breakfast she cleaned her teeth.

5 It takes John twenty minutes to walk to school.

6 Sally wrote the letter and James posted it.

7 I looked for my badge but it had disappeared.

8 The old man flopped down in the armchair and grunted.

B Fit the verbs in the list on the left into their proper places in the sentences below.

1 Miss Haines _____ the children to the party.

2 Patch _____ at the food before eating it.

3 Sheila _____ across the moor on her pony.

4 The worms _____ about in the rain.

5 William _____ the holes in the fence.

6 The rain _____ down the window panes.

7 Some of the audience _____ their feet.

8 The runaway horses had _____ on all the flowers in the park.

Adjectives

Anne wore a **pretty silk** dress.

The words **pretty** and **silk** tell us something about Anne's dress.

Because they describe the noun dress, they are called **adjectives**.

A word which describes a noun is called an adjective.

valuable
thrilling
fashionable
nourishing
fatal
loyal
stormy
savage
tedious
happy

A Make a list of the adjectives in these sentences.

Example 1 cold wet

1 It was a cold, wet night.

2 The little children played in the bright, warm sunshine.

3 The ancient castle was surrounded by a deep moat.

4 Hard work made him a successful man.

5 Celia was slim and graceful, with blue eyes and golden hair.

6 Huge waves were making the giant liner roll.

7 Grandpa enjoys sitting by a warm fire in his comfortable armchair.

8 It was a delicious cake covered in thick chocolate icing.

B Use the ten adjectives in the list on the left to complete the phrases below:

1 a _____ meal
2 a _____ sea
3 a _____ child
4 a _____ ring
5 a _____ accident
6 a _____ hat
7 a _____ dog
8 a _____ story
9 a _____ task
10 a _____ friend

C Write five sentences of your own using any of the completed phrases above. Phrases 5 and 8 have been used in the examples below.

A fatal accident occurred at the corner of the High Street last night.

Roger read a thrilling story about pirates.

3

Nouns formation

Verb	Noun
admire	admiration
begin	beginning
compose	composition
depart	departure
describe	description
divide	division
exist	existence
inform	information
intend	intention
invent	invention
laugh	laughter
lose	loss
move	movement
perform	performance
permit	permission
persuade	persuasion
please	pleasure
rebel	rebellion
serve	service
settle	settlement

A   Write the missing nouns which are formed from the verbs in bold type.

1   a clever _____   **invent**
2   helpful _____   **inform**
3   hearty _____   **laugh**
4   a brilliant _____   **perform**
5   a serious _____   **lose**
6   faithful _____   **serve**
7   simple _____   **divide**
8   a good _____   **begin**
9   a life of _____   **please**
10 an early _____   **settle**

B   Give the noun formed from the verb in bold type, which will complete each sentence.

1   The injured man found the least ____ very painful.   **move**

2   It is our ____ to visit Greece next year.   **intend**

3   Bad weather delayed the ____ of the plane.   **depart**

4   Alan received ____ to leave school early.   **permit**

5   The boy wrote an excellent ____ about dogs.   **compose**

6   I have a deep ____ for the artist's work.   **admire**

7   A hermit leads a very lonely ____ .   **exist**

8   Many were killed in the ____ against the government.   **rebel**

9   *Treasure Island* contains a splendid ____ of Long John Silver.   **describe**

10 After a little ____ Simon agreed to lend the boys his new football.   **persuade**

Nouns number

Singular means **one**.

Plural means **more than one**.

Singular	Plural
girl	girls
book	books
class	classes
leaf	leaves
lily	lilies
hero	heroes

Some nouns keep the same spelling for both singular and plural:

deer	swine
salmon	trout
sheep	

These nouns have no **singular** form.

trousers	tongs
scissors	bellows
shears	tweezers

A   Write the plural form for each of the singular nouns below. Follow the instructions on the left of each group.

	Singular	Plural
Add **-s**	chief	____
	chimney	____
	piano	____
	roof	____
Add **-es**	cargo	____
	echo	____
	hero	____
	potato	____
	tomato	____
Change **y** to **i**, add **-es**	battery	____
	hobby	____
	reply	____
	supply	____
Change **f** to **v**, add **es**	half	____
	leaf	____
	loaf	____
	shelf	____
	wolf	____
Change the vowels	foot	____
	goose	____
Use your dictionary	mouse	____
	tooth	____
	woman	____

B   Write the **plural** form of each noun.

1	half	5	bully	9	piano
2	hobby	6	tomato	10	wolf
3	potato	7	leaf	11	reply
4	sheep	8	chimney	12	goose

C   Write the **singular** form of each noun.

1	feet	5	mice	9	toes
2	heroes	6	shelves	10	teeth
3	loaves	7	echoes	11	batteries
4	supplies	8	women	12	swines

5

Sinbad and the coconuts

One day a merchant gave me a large bag and advised me to go picking coconuts with some men whom we met in a place much visited by foreign traders. I kept close to the party until we reached the place where the coconuts grew.

The trees were so tall that I wondered how we should get the nuts, when the men, picking up some stones, threw them at the monkeys, of whom there were many on the branches. These creatures in return pelted us with coconuts, throwing them down so quickly that we soon filled our bags.

Day after day this was done until at length we had enough to fill the ship which waited for us in the harbour. Then, bidding the friendly merchant good-bye, I went aboard, and in due time arrived in Baghdad, none the worse for my adventures. I had done well, too, with my coconuts, having changed them for pearls and spices in the places at which we had called on the voyage.

The Arabian Nights

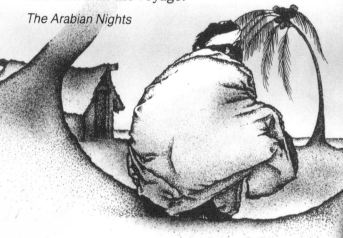

1 What did one of the merchants give Sinbad to carry the coconuts in?
2 Why did Sinbad wonder how they would get the coconuts off the trees?
3 What did the men throw at the monkeys on the branches of the trees?
4 What did the monkeys throw at the men in return?
5 What did the men do with the things the monkeys threw at them?
6 For how long did this throwing continue?
7 Where did Sinbad's voyage end?
8 In what way had Sinbad done well with his coconuts?

Verbs past tense and participle

Learn the **past tense** and the **participles** of the ten verbs in the first column, then do the exercises.

Present tense	Past tense	Participle
beat	beat	beaten
bleed	bled	bled
catch	caught	caught
forget	forgot	forgotten
hold	held	held
shake	shook	shaken
strike	struck	struck
swim	swam	swum
throw	threw	thrown
write	wrote	written

A participle always needs a helping word.

Example
The girls **were shaken** by their fall.

The word **were** helps the participle **shaken**.

Learn the following helping words:

was	have been
had	has been
were	had been

A Fill each space with the past tense of the verb in bold type.

1 Philip _____ from the beach to the boat. **swim**

2 Arsenal _____ Chelsea by two goals to nil. **beat**

3 The Queen _____ hands with the General. **shake**

4 Roger _____ a letter to his uncle. **write**

5 His nose _____ badly when he fell. **bleed**

6 Stephen _____ the long pole with both hands. **hold**

B Use the **participle** of the verb in bold type to fill each space. The helping words are underlined.

1 The rider <u>was</u> _____ by his horse. **throw**

2 Donald <u>had</u> _____ to post the letters. **forget**

3 Chelsea <u>were</u> _____ by Arsenal. **beat**

4 Many books <u>have been</u> _____ about Napoleon. **write**

5 The English Channel <u>has been</u> _____ many times. **swim**

6 The old man <u>had been</u> _____ by his fall. **shake**

Comparing adjectives

Compare the heights of these three boys.

John is **tall**.

Alan is **taller** than John.

Richard is the **tallest**.

taller is used in comparing **two**

tallest is used in comparing **more**

In the examples above **-er** and **-est** have been added to the word tall to show the comparative height of each boy.

There are many adjectives where **-er** and **-est** can be added without any change in spelling.

| cold | colder | coldest |
| clean | cleaner | cleanest |

But look out for these spelling changes.

Drop **e** at the end

| nice | nicer | nicest |
| fine | finer | finest |

Change the **y** to **i**

| lazy | lazier | laziest |
| shady | shadier | shadiest |

Double the last letter

| thin | thinner | thinnest |
| slim | slimmer | slimmest |

John   Alan   Richard

Use the correct form of the adjective in bold type to complete each sentence.

1   The monk's habit was made of the ____ material I have ever seen.   **coarse**

2   This is the ____ classroom in the school.   **cold**

3   Miss Agnes is the ____ of the two sisters.   **slim**

4   King Solomon was the ____ king who ever reigned.   **wise**

5   Only the ____ ingredients are used in our cakes.   **pure**

6   Jane chose the ____ slice of cake on the dish.   **thin**

7   High Street is a much ____ street than West Street.   **wide**

8   Brighton is one of our ____ seaside resorts.   **sunny**

9   Colin is the ____ of the twins.   **big**

10   The oak is a ____ tree than the poplar.   **shady**

Words to complete words

A   Complete each unfinished word in these sentences by writing a word of **three letters** in place of the dashes at the beginning.

Example   1   **bat**   **bat**ch

1   The baker put another _ _ _ch of bread in the oven.

2   Turn off the light. Do not _ _ _te electricity.

3   A party of children sang Christmas _ _ _ols to the old people.

4   It did not take the police long to _ _ _ture the escaped convict.

5   The groceries are kept in a kitchen _ _ _board.

6   He did not add up the _ _ _ures correctly.

7   Some _ _ _tle were grazing in the field.

8   The footballer scored from a _ _ _alty kick.

9   One stag had broken an _ _ _ler in the fight.

10   The conjurer made the handkerchief _ _ _ish.

B   Complete each unfinished word below by writing a word of three letters in place of the dashes at the end.

Example   1   **den**   bur**den**

1   A big bur_ _ _ was placed on the camel's back.

2   Roy used a mag_ _ _ to pick up the nails he had dropped.

3   One of the knights was killed in the com_ _ _ _.

4   Mandy felt very tired after her swimming les_ _ _.

5   The frog gave a loud cr_ _ _ and hopped away.

6   King John was a tyr_ _ _ _.

7   The sudden light made him bl_ _ _ his eyes.

8   The gunners were right on the tar_ _ _.

9   Jill did not man_ _ _ to finish her homework.

10   The floor of the lounge was covered with thick car_ _ _.

9

Using words correctly

Passed

I asked Ken to **pass** the jam.
Ken **passed** the jam.

Past

It is **past** ten o'clock.
We walked **past** the new shop.
He had been ill for the **past** few days.

Past often follows a verb, like ran **past**, flew **past**, went **past**, marched **past**, etc.

It's means **It is**.
The **'** shows that the **i** in **is** has been left out.

Its means '**belonging to it**'.
Its shows **possession**.

A Copy these sentences, filling each blank with **past** or **passed**.

1 Helen ＿＿＿ the cakes to Angela.

2 It was ten minutes ＿＿＿ two when the train arrived.

3 Margaret ＿＿＿ her music examination with honours.

4 The colonel saluted as he ＿＿＿ the Union Jack.

5 The colonel saluted as he marched ＿＿＿ the Union Jack.

6 William hopes to do better in the future than he has done in the ＿＿＿ .

7 On the last lap David ＿＿＿ all the other competitors and won easily.

8 On the last lap David sprinted ＿＿＿ all the other competitors and won easily.

B Copy these sentences, inserting **it's** or **its**, as required.

1 The rook flapped ＿＿＿ wings and flew off.

2 I think ＿＿＿ going to be a fine day.

3 Father says ＿＿＿ a long journey to London.

4 The little lamb frisked round ＿＿＿ mother.

5 The kangaroo carries ＿＿＿ young in a pouch.

6 Farmer Gray says ＿＿＿ cold enough to snow.

7 The dog hurt ＿＿＿ paw yesterday, but ＿＿＿ all right now.

8 Paul said ＿＿＿ time the puppy had ＿＿＿ food.

Alphabetical order

A Write the names of the eight objects in this picture in alphabetical order.

B Arrange the words in each group in alphabetical order. Look at the **first** letter of each word.

1	doubt	2	justice	3	month
	youth		grab		unicorn
	broad		kneel		skilful
	active		chemist		nothing
	lenient		eastern		haughty

C Look at the **second** letter of each word when arranging them alphabetically.

1	plank	2	clever	3	grape
	press		crisp		geese
	panic		centre		guilty
	punch		canter		gander
	perch		cheat		goose

D Look at the **third** letter of each word when arranging each group in alphabetical order.

1	decide	2	harmful	3	prune
	demand		habit		prepare
	deadly		haunt		produce
	defeat		hatch		price
	debtor		hamper		prank

The crows and the snake

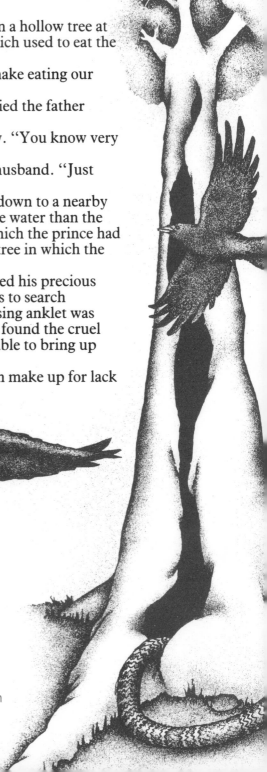

Long ago, in India, a pair of crows nested in a hollow tree at the bottom of which lived a fierce snake which used to eat the young birds as soon as they were hatched.

"Oh dear, how can we stop this horrid snake eating our children?" said the mother crow one day.

"We must get rid of him, my dear," replied the father crow.

"But that is impossible," said Mrs. Crow. "You know very well that he is much stronger than we are."

"Don't worry, my dear," answered her husband. "Just leave everything to me."

The following day the king's son came down to a nearby river to swim. No sooner had he entered the water than the father crow seized the lovely gold anklet which the prince had taken off and dropped it inside the hollow tree in which the crows had their nest.

When he was dressing, the prince noticed his precious anklet was missing and ordered his servants to search everywhere for it. After some time the missing anklet was found in the hollow tree. The servants also found the cruel snake and killed it, and so the crows were able to bring up their next family in peace.

This fable teaches us that skill will often make up for lack of strength.

1 Why were the crows unable to bring up a family?
2 Why did the mother crow think that they could not get rid of their enemy?
3 Who came down to the river the following day?
4 Why did he come?
5 What did the crow take when the prince was swimming?
6 Where did he hide it?
7 What did the servants find in addition to what they were looking for?
8 Why were the crows able to bring up their family in peace after this?

Gender

A **boy** is a **male**

A **girl** is a **female**

The grouping of words according to sex is called **gender**.

Nouns which name **males** belong to the **masculine** gender.

Nouns which name **females** belong to the **feminine** gender.

Masculine	Feminine
actor	actress
bridegroom	bride
cockerel	hen
dog	bitch
duke	duchess
earl	countess
emperor	empress
fox	vixen
gander	goose
headmaster	headmistress
hero	heroine
landlord	landlady
monk	nun
host	hostess
prince	princess
son	daughter
stallion	mare
tiger	tigress

A   Write the **feminine** gender of:

1   hero
2   dog
3   fox
4   monk
5   prince
6   earl
7   actor
8   son
9   headmaster
10   host
11   stallion
12   emperor

B   Write the **masculine** gender of:

1   actress
2   bride
3   goose
4   hen
5   empress
6   landlady
7   mare
8   headmistress
9   tigress
10   duchess
11   vixen
12   nun

C   Change each noun of the **masculine** gender to the **feminine** gender.

1   The duke is eighty years old.

2   As the children passed, the gander hissed at them.

3   The rider led the stallion to the stable.

4   We were welcomed by the landlord of The Swan Hotel.

D   Write the word which is missing from each sentence.

1   The _____ and countess are abroad on holiday.

2   There were three hens and a _____ in the farmyard.

3   The _____ waited in vain for the bride to arrive at the church.

4   There were four puppies, one bitch and three _____ .

Letter writing

Points to remember:

1 Write freely, as if you were actually **speaking** to the person to whom you are writing.

2 Write plainly and neatly.

3 See that your spelling is correct. If in doubt, use a dictionary.

4 Use a suitable ending.

Parent	Love
Friend	Yours ever
	All the best
	Love
Cousin	Best wishes
	Love

5 Address your envelope fully and plainly, so that the postman will have no difficulty in delivering it.

Here are some suggestions for letters, but you may choose something else if you wish.

Write a letter to:

1 a friend who has moved to another town and has just written to you.

2 an uncle, thanking him for a birthday present he has sent you.

3 a friend, describing a seaside holiday you are enjoying.

4 a cousin, inviting him or her to spend a holiday at your home.

5 a friend who is in hospital.

6 your mother, thanking her for a parcel she has sent you whilst you are away from home.

7 a friend, congratulating him or her on passing an examination.

8 a new penfriend, describing yourself, your family and your interests.

Adjectives formation

Many adjectives are formed by adding the letter **y** to a noun.

Examples

greed	greedy
rust	rusty
health	healthy

In the examples above, **y** can be added to the noun without any change in spelling.

But look out for the following changes.

If the noun ends with **e**, this letter is dropped before the **y** is added.

Examples

bone	bony
noise	noisy
haste	hasty

When **y** is added to some nouns the last letter is doubled.

Examples

fur	furry
mud	muddy
skin	skinny

A   Form adjectives from the nouns in bold type. No change.

1   A person with a great **thirst** is _____ .

2   A child who is longing to **sleep** is _____ .

3   Fingers stained with **ink** are _____ .

4   A sky with a lot of **cloud** is _____ .

5   A loaf with a crisp **crust** is _____ .

6   A sea with a **storm** raging is _____ .

B   Form adjectives from the nouns in bold type. Drop the **e**.

1   Water which is as cold as **ice** is _____ .

2   Cheeks like a **rose** are _____ .

3   An orange full of **juice** is _____ .

4   A tree which provides **shade** is _____ .

5   A chimney which pours out **smoke** is _____ .

6   Hands covered with **grease** are _____ .

C   Form adjectives from the nouns in bold type. Double the last letter.

1   A road covered with **mud** is _____ .

2   A garden which gets much **sun** is _____ .

3   Foods which contain a lot of **fat** are _____ .

4   A day when there is a lot of **fog** is _____ .

5   Trousers which are as loose as a **bag** are _____ .

6   A story which causes **fun** is _____ .

Same sound — different meaning

The words in each pair are pronounced alike but are different in spelling and meaning.

ball anything round; a large party for dancing

bawl to shout loudly

bean a vegetable; a plant

been e.g. has been; have been

flour finely ground wheat

flower a blossom

grate a fireplace; to scrape

great large; important

him e.g. Let him come

hymn a song of praise

hole an open place

whole all of it; complete

leak escape of gas, water, etc.

leek a vegetable

mail posted letters; armour

male e.g. Boys and men are males

peace quiet; stillness; freedom from war

piece a bit or part

A Choose the correct word from the pair above to complete each sentence.

1 **flower   flour**
The cook used self-raising ____ for the cakes.

2 **whole   hole**
The greedy boy ate the ____ cake himself.

3 **whole   hole**
The ____ in the pipe was soon mended.

4 **great   grate**
The strong wind made the door ____ on its hinges.

5 **peace   piece**
The mouse nibbled the ____ of cheese.

B To complete each sentence below you need a pair of words from the list. Be sure to put each word in the right place.

1 The cook had ____ slicing runner ____ for two hours.

2 Nobody got any ____ until the baby was given a ____ of chocolate.

3 John was pleased when the music teacher asked ____ to play the organ for the morning ____ .

4 The little boy started to ____ when the dog ran off with his rubber ____ .

People

ancestor	A person from whom one is descended.
bachelor	An unmarried man.
bankrupt	Is unable to pay his debts.
blackleg	A person who refuses to join a strike.
bully	Teases and ill-treats those weaker than himself.
guest	A person received and entertained at another's house.
host	The person who entertains the guests. *Feminine* – hostess
orphan	A child whose parents are dead.
volunteer	Offers to serve of his own free will.
widow	A woman whose husband is dead.
widower	A man whose wife is dead.

Learn the words in the list above, and their meanings, then answer the questions below.

A Give one word for each of the following.

1 One who gives a service without being compelled to.

2 A man whose wife has died and who has not remarried.

3 A business man who has £50 and owes £5,000.

4 A child whose parents are dead.

5 A woman who invites friends to parties at her home.

B Use one word to complete each sentence.

1 Simon disliked women and was determined to remain a _____.

2 The Duke of Marlborough, who won the Battle of Blenheim, was an _____ of Sir Winston Churchill.

3 Crowds of strikers booed the _____ as they entered the factory.

4 The _____ hurt the little boy and made him cry.

5 The _____ thanked their host for a wonderful party.

The Princess and the pea

There was once a Prince who wanted to marry a real Princess. He travelled all over the world looking for one, but failed to find one, so he returned home.

One night, during a terrible storm, there was a knocking at the gate of the town, and the old King went to open it. It was a Princess who stood outside. And, oh dear! what a state she was in. The water ran down from her hair and her clothes into her shoes, but she said she was a real Princess.

"Well, that we'll soon find out," thought the Queen, but she said nothing. Instead she went into the bedroom and laid a small pea on the slabs of the bed. Upon these she heaped twenty mattresses and twenty eiderdown beds. The Princess was to sleep there that night.

In the morning she was asked how she had slept.

"Oh, very badly," she answered. "I have scarcely closed my eyes all night. I lay on something hard, so that my body is all black and blue."

Everybody knew then that she was a real Princess because no one else would have felt the pea through all those soft mattresses and eiderdown beds, and so the Prince married her.

1   What did the Prince wish to do?
2   What was heard during the storm?
3   Who went to open the gate?
4   Who stood outside the gate?
5   What small thing did the Queen put on the slabs of the bed?
6   What did she put on top of this?
7   How did the Princess sleep that night?
8   What was her body like next morning?

Collective nouns

Some nouns name a **group** or **collection** of things.
These are called **collective nouns**.

bees	swarm
books	library
cows	herd
china	set
corn	sheaf
elephants	herd
fish	shoal
friends	party
furniture	suite
islands	group
kittens	litter
musicians	group
monkeys	troop
soldiers	regiment
oxen	team
flowers	bunch
thieves	gang
whales	school

A   Write the missing words.

1 a _____ of china
2 a _____ of corn
3 a _____ of friends
4 a _____ of elephants
5 a _____ of flowers
6 a _____ of thieves
7 a _____ of books
8 a _____ of bees

9 a school of _____
10 a team of _____
11 a shoal of _____
12 a suite of _____
13 a herd of _____
14 a troop of _____
15 a litter of _____
16 a group of _____

B   Write the collective nouns which are missing from these sentences.

1 The look-out sighted a _____ of whales in the distance.

2 A _____ of thieves held up the mail van and robbed it.

3 The explorer took photographs of a _____ of elephants.

4 A _____ of fish was approaching the trawler.

5 Each room in the hotel had a new _____ of furniture.

6 The heavy wagon was drawn by a _____ of oxen.

7 The Orkneys are a _____ of islands off Northern Scotland.

8 A _____ of bees had settled on an apple tree in the orchard.

9 The tabby cat was very proud of her _____ of kittens.

Forming adjectives from nouns

Noun	Adjective
affection	affectionate
anger	angry
centre	central
courage	courageous
custom	customary
danger	dangerous
expense	expensive
fame	famous
favour	favourite
friend	friendly
fury	furious
haste	hasty
hero	heroic
marvel	marvellous
music	musical
nature	natural
poison	poisonous
value	valuable
victory	victorious
wool	woollen

A What are the adjectives formed from these nouns?

1	wool	11	anger
2	haste	12	marvel
3	favour	13	custom
4	nature	14	music
5	poison	15	danger
6	affection	16	expense
7	fury	17	courage
8	hero	18	friend
9	victory	19	fame
10	centre	20	value

B Write the adjective, formed from the noun in bold type, which will complete each sentence.

1 The captain's ____ conduct saved the lives of his crew. **hero**

2 My ____ book is *Watership Down*. **favour**

3 The Niagara Falls are a ____ sight. **marvel**

4 The thieves stole a ____ diamond necklace. **value**

5 The lady bought a very ____ fur coat. **expense**

6 Grandpa was seated in his ____ armchair. **custom**

7 Some plants bear ____ berries. **poison**

8 Marcia's hair has ____ waves. **nature**

9 Judith is a very ____ child. **affection**

10 The lost boy was helped by a ____ policeman. **friend**

100%
WOOL

Pronouns

a I lent Paul a book and **Paul** lost the **book**.

b I lent Paul a book and **he** lost **it**.

Instead of repeating the word **Paul**, the word **he** is used in **b**. Instead of repeating the word **book**, the word **it** is used.

A word which is used instead of a noun is called a pronoun.

Look at these pronouns:

I	me
you	you
he	him
she	her
it	it
we	us
they	them

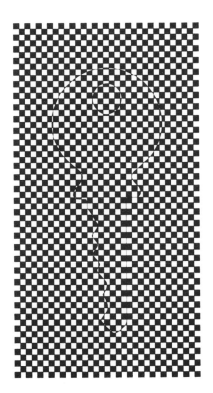

A Rewrite these sentences, using **pronouns** in place of the nouns in bold type.

1 Alan told Charles that **Alan** would help **Charles**.

2 The rabbit ran away when **the rabbit** heard a dog barking.

3 Anne and Janet said that **Anne and Janet** would call again.

4 Mrs. Grey has two poodles. **Mrs. Grey** adores **the two poodles**.

5 Enid promised June that **Enid** would feed the dog for **June**.

B Make a list of the pronouns in these sentences.

1 David's mother gave him a bar of chocolate.

2 Wendy complained that she was very tired.

3 Our teacher told us that we must come to school early.

4 Would you like another cup of tea, Rosemary?

5 Michael told Mary that he would help her find her key.

6 The captain told the sailor to put his cap on straight.

Fun with words

A   In each group below, the second word of each pair is formed by writing a letter **before** the first word. A different letter is used for each group. Look at the letter that is added and write the missing words.

Example					
	ash	dash		ash	**d**ash
	one	done		one	**d**one
	rip	____		rip	**d**rip

In this group the letter **d** is added.

1	ale	tale	2	end	send	3	ice	rice
	ray	tray		ink	sink		oar	roar
	wine	____		old	____		each	____

4	hip	whip	5	oil	boil	6	age	page
	arm	warm		lame	blame		our	pour
	edge	____		rain	____		lace	____

7	hop	chop	8	air	fair	9	elf	self
	lap	clap		owl	fowl		kid	skid
	rash	____		lock	____		hark	____

B   The first line of each pair below has a code word and its meaning. The same code is used in the second line of each example. You have to find out what this means.

Example   1   **ijou** means **hint**
                 uijo means **thin**

Using the code for the word **hint** we can find the meaning of the letters **uijo**.

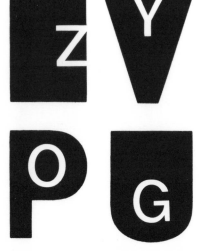

1   **ijou** means **hint**
    uijo means ____

2   **ujef** means **tide**
    ejfu means ____

3   **dbsf** means **care**
    sbdf means ____

4   **bdut** means **acts**
    dbtu means ____

5   **ivct** means **hubs**
    cvti means ____

6   **ebmf** means **dale**
    mfbe means ____

7   **nbsdi** means **march**
    dibsn means ____

8   **qfubm** means **petal**
    mfbqu means ____

9   **tufbm** means **steal**
    mfbtu means ____

10   **qjtupm** means **pistol**
     tqpjmu means ____

Using capital letters

Capital letters are used:

to begin every sentence	**T**he pirate wore a big gold earring
to begin every line of poetry	**H**e thought he saw a Buffalo **U**pon the chimney-piece;
for the names of people and pets, and for initials	**M**ary, **H**arold, **S**pot, **F**luffy, **A. J. C**ompton
for the names of places, rivers, mountains, etc.	**L**ondon, **S**nowdon, **T**hames, **W**indermere
in writing addresses	23 **S**econd **A**venue, **H**opsham, **S**ussex
for the names of well-known buildings	**T**he **N**ational **G**allery, **T**he **B**ritish **M**useum, **W**indsor **C**astle
for the names of days, months and holidays	**T**hursday, **J**anuary, **E**aster, **G**ood **F**riday
for the names of books, poems, songs, newspapers, etc.	**K**idnapped, **W**atership **D**own, **T**he **T**imes
for the word **I**	~~W~~hen **I** bought it **I** thought **I** had a bargain.

A   Rewrite these sentences using capital letters where required.

1   ian saw the houses of parliament and buckingham palace.

2   i shall be on holiday on saturday the 29th of july.

3   we are moving to 24 richmond road, swansea.

4   if all the seas were one sea,
    what a great sea that would be!

5   easter monday is the monday after good friday

6   jean has read oliver twist and black beauty.

B   Write the following:

1   three first names
2   three surnames
3   the names of three days
4   the title of any book

Aladdin

In one of the large cities of China there once lived a tailor, whose name was Mustapha. Mustapha was very poor, and found it hard to provide food for himself, his wife, and his only child, Aladdin.

Aladdin was a very naughty and lazy boy. He would never do what his parents wanted him to do, but played in the streets from morning till night with boys who were as naughty as himself.

When Aladdin was old enough to learn a trade his father took him into his own shop and began to show him how to use a needle. It was no use. Aladdin had had his own way so long that he could not settle down to work. His father tried him over and over again, and was at last so angry and upset at his son's idle habits that he became ill and soon died.

The poor widow thought that her son would now earn a little money, but he would not. Aladdin was as idle as ever. In despair, she sold all the things that were in the shop, and with this money and the little she earnt by spinning cotton she got on fairly well.

The Arabian Nights

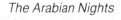

1 Where did Mustapha live?
2 What was his occupation?
3 How many children did he have?
4 Name three of Aladdin's faults.
5 What did Aladdin do all day?
6 What did Mustapha do when Aladdin was old enough to learn a trade?
7 Why could Aladdin not settle down to work?
8 What effect did Aladdin's idle habits have on Mustapha?
9 What did Aladdin's mother do with the things in the tailor's shop?
10 How did Aladdin's mother earn money after her husband's death?

Direct speech

''What is the matter with your hand?'' asked Nigel.

The words actually spoken by Nigel were:

What is the matter with your hand?

This is called **direct speech**.

These words are always written inside speech marks, or inverted commas " "

The first commas " are placed **just before the first word spoken**.

The last commas " are placed **just after the last word spoken**.

A   Copy the following sentences, putting in the **speech marks**.
Remember that '' comes after the comma or question mark, never before or above.

1   Pass me the butter, Carol, said her mother.

2   Would you like another cake? asked Mrs. Brown.

3   These eggs are not fresh, complained the customer.

4   Is this the way to Norfolk, please? inquired the walker.

5   Look out below, shouted the steeplejack.

6   Please do all you can to help us, cried Old Tom.

7   The meeting is now closed, declared the chairman.

8   Pick your feet up, the sergeant-major shouted to the recruits.

9   I am the best bowler in the team, boasted Andrew.

10   Don't let me catch you throwing stones again, Peter, warned his father.

B   Write four sentences containing **direct speech** about:

1   something you said to one of your friends.

2   something your teacher has told your class to do.

3   anything you have asked your father or mother.

Occupations

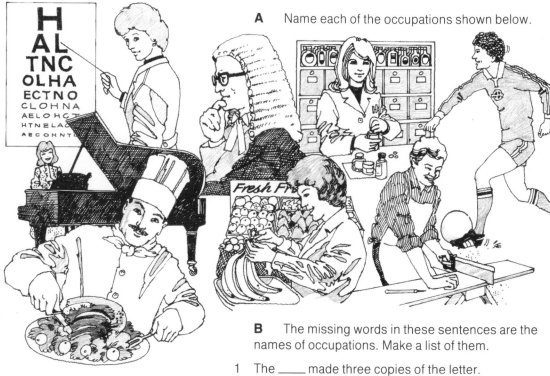

A Name each of the occupations shown below.

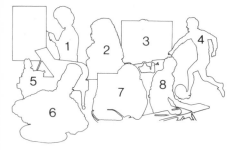

B The missing words in these sentences are the names of occupations. Make a list of them.

1 The ____ made three copies of the letter.

2 The ____ sentenced the prisoner to six months imprisonment.

3 Jackson has scored more goals than any other ____ this season.

4 This picture was painted by a famous ____ .

5 The ____ told Andrew he needed glasses.

6 The ____ stood at the top of the gangway and welcomed the passengers aboard the aeroplane.

air hostess
artist
butcher
carpenter
chef
chemist
conductor
confectioner
fishmonger
footballer

fruiterer
grocer
jockey
judge
optician
photographer
pianist
policewoman
typist

C What name is given to a person who sells:

1 apples, pears, plums?

2 chocolates and sweets?

3 herrings, cod, hake?

4 pills, medicines, ointments?

5 pork, beef, mutton?

6 flour, cheese, bacon?

Proper adjectives

Learn these adjectives which are formed from the names of countries. Notice that each begins with a capital letter.

Country	Adjective
Britain	British
Canada	Canadian
England	English
Egypt	Egyptian
France	French
Germany	German
Ireland	Irish
Italy	Italian
Japan	Japanese
Russia	Russian
Scotland	Scottish
Wales	Welsh

A What are the missing adjectives?

1 The Highlands of Scotland   the ____ Highlands

2 Goods made in Britain   ____ goods

3 Butter made in Ireland   ____ butter

4 A farmhouse in England   an ____ farmhouse

5 The language of France   the ____ language

6 Cotton grown in Egypt   ____ cotton

7 Ballet music of Russia   ____ ballet music

B In each line the missing word is the adjective formed from the name of the country in bold type.

1 Britain imports large quantities of ____ peaches. **Italy**

2 The travellers were stopped at the ____ frontier. **Germany**

3 Two girls were dressed in ____ costume. **Japan**

4 A great welcome awaited Solzhenitsyn, the ____ writer. **Russia**

5 ____ apples have a fine flavour. **Canada**

6 In the museum there is an ____ mummy. **Egypt.**

7 The tourists spent a week in Paris, the ____ capital. **France**

C Write six sentences of your own, each of which contains one of the adjectives formed from the names of these countries.

1 Wales   4 England
2 France   5 Ireland
3 Scotland   6 Britain

Using words correctly revision

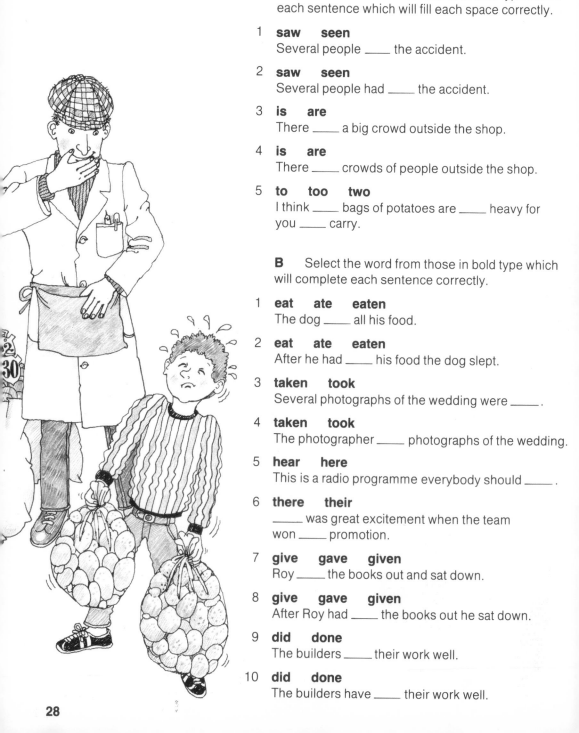

A Select the word from those in bold type above each sentence which will fill each space correctly.

1 **saw   seen**
Several people _____ the accident.

2 **saw   seen**
Several people had _____ the accident.

3 **is   are**
There _____ a big crowd outside the shop.

4 **is   are**
There _____ crowds of people outside the shop.

5 **to   too   two**
I think _____ bags of potatoes are _____ heavy for you _____ carry.

B Select the word from those in bold type which will complete each sentence correctly.

1 **eat   ate   eaten**
The dog _____ all his food.

2 **eat   ate   eaten**
After he had _____ his food the dog slept.

3 **taken   took**
Several photographs of the wedding were _____.

4 **taken   took**
The photographer _____ photographs of the wedding.

5 **hear   here**
This is a radio programme everybody should _____.

6 **there   their**
_____ was great excitement when the team won _____ promotion.

7 **give   gave   given**
Roy _____ the books out and sat down.

8 **give   gave   given**
After Roy had _____ the books out he sat down.

9 **did   done**
The builders _____ their work well.

10 **did   done**
The builders have _____ their work well.

Group names

buildings
counties
entertainments
games
headgear
letters
months
numbers
occupations
rivers
seasons
weapons

A   Write the **group name** for the three things in each of the columns below. Look at the words in the list on the left.

1   summer
     winter
     spring

2   sword
     rifle
     bomb

3   m t h
     l z e
     r q k

4   Kent
     Surrey
     Yorkshire

5   circus
     cinema
     theatre

6   4   9   1
     12 35 67

7   carpenter
     miner
     farmer

8   Thames
     Severn
     Humber

9   cap
     hat
     beret

10 April
     August
     March

11 draughts
     chess
     dominoes

12 hospital
     school
     museum

B   In each column below choose the word which is the **group name** for all the other words.

1   fly
     wasp
     insect
     bee
     gnat

2   skylark
     swallow
     robin
     bird
     sparrow

3   giraffe
     animal
     tiger
     elephant
     leopard

C   Draw four columns and write the headings:

Fish	**Flowers**	**Groceries**	**Trees**

Then place the words below in their correct columns. There will be six words in each group.

beech
tea
daffodil
salmon
butter
snowdrop
lard
elm
hake
bluebell
oak
mackerel
herring
daisy
ash
cheese
tulip
birch
pansy
plaice
sugar
sycamore
cod
margarine

A find for Carlos

The brindle puppy wandered on a little further, coming to a crack in the ground which was lined with a few blades of grass and wild flowers. A trickle of water drew her attention and at this she lapped, after half choking herself before realising how to use her tongue, and then she curled up on a patch of grass which had dried in the sun and fell asleep.

It was there that Carlos found her later that afternoon. He lived in a block of flats beyond the cottages and had wandered that way out of sheer curiosity and boredom. Too new to the district to have made any friends, time lay heavily on his hands that Sunday afternoon. He was thirteen, too young according to his sixteen-year-old brother to share his pursuits; lonely.

He found the crack in the ground along which the narrow, dirty stream trickled and because there was a little bit of grass and a few flowers, he thought there might be frogs or lizards or something. When he first saw the brindle puppy he thought she was dead, but then he saw the tiny flanks heave and picked her up, his heart jumping with excitement at his find.

The deserted place, her bedraggled condition, made him sure that she belonged to no one. He pushed her inside his anorak and turned for home, his instinct being to get away from the place as soon as possible, just in case someone came for her.

Just a Dog   Helen Griffiths

1   How can you tell that the puppy was a very young one?
2   What buildings did Carlos pass on his way to the puppy?
3   Why had Carlos wandered out that afternoon?
4   Why had he not made any friends?
5   Why did Carlos' brother not want his company?
6   What did Carlos expect to find in the crack?
7   Why did he expect to find these?
8   How did he know the puppy was alive?
9   Why did he feel sure that the puppy had no owner?
10 Why did he want to leave that place as soon as possible?

Joining sentences

Jill ate her supper.
She went to bed.

two sentences

Jill ate her supper **and** went to bed.

one sentence

Ian looked everywhere for his cap.
He could not find it.

Ian looked everywhere for his cap **but** could not find it.

It was raining heavily.
We stayed indoors.

It was raining heavily **so** we stayed indoors.

Tim was happy.
It was his birthday.

Tim was happy **because** it was his birthday.

A Use **and** to join each pair of sentences.

1 Katy washed the car.
   She polished it until it shone.

2 John took off his shoes and socks.
   John paddled in the sea.

3 The goalkeeper jumped high.
   He punched the ball away.

B Use **but** to join each pair of sentences.

1 The dog chased the cat.
   He failed to catch her.

2 She slipped and fell.
   She did not hurt herself.

3 Fire destroyed the factory.
   No lives were lost.

C Use **so** to join each pair of sentences.

1 The tap was frozen.
   We could get no water.

2 He could not spell the word.
   He looked it up in his dictionary.

3 Jane had measles.
   She could not go to the party.

4 Stephen spent his bus fare on sweets.
   He had to walk home.

D Use **and**, **but**, **so** or **because** to join each pair of sentences.

1 He could not walk.
   He had sprained his ankle.

2 David had a bad headache.
   He went to bed early.

3 Louise went to the dentist.
   She had two teeth filled.

4 I enjoy going swimming.
   I do not like cold water.

Opposites using un, in, im

The opposite of certain words can be formed by adding **un**, **in**, or **im**.

Adding un

certain	uncertain
comfortable	uncomfortable
common	uncommon
conscious	unconscious
healthy	unhealthy
pleasant	unpleasant
selfish	unselfish
steady	unsteady
suitable	unsuitable
truthful	untruthful
used	unused
wise	unwise

Adding in or im

capable	incapable
complete	incomplete
convenient	inconvenient
correct	incorrect
curable	incurable
direct	indirect
secure	insecure
sufficient	insufficient
visible	invisible
movable	immovable
possible	impossible
pure	impure

A Write the opposites of these words.

1	secure	11	sufficient
2	selfish	12	healthy
3	pure	13	movable
4	common	14	used
5	capable	15	visible
6	certain	16	steady
7	direct	17	possible
8	pleasant	18	suitable
9	convenient	19	wise
10	correct	20	complete

B Which word in your list of opposites best describes:

1 a person who frequently tells lies?

2 a salary which is not enough to live on?

3 something which cannot be seen?

4 a person who is frequently ill?

5 a person who puts others before himself?

6 a pack of cards from which some are missing?

7 a rock which cannot be moved?

8 a disease which cannot be cured?

9 a sum in which there is a mistake?

10 a person who has fainted?

People

cannibal	Eats human flesh.
coward	Lacks courage; is afraid.
daredevil	Is recklessly daring.
glutton	A person who overeats.
hermit	A person living in isolation from others.
martyr	A person forced to suffer or die for a belief.
miser	Lives sparingly in order to hoard money.
patriot	A person who loves and wishes to serve his country.
pilgrim	Travels to a sacred place as a religious devotion.
spendthrift	Spends money unnecessarily.
truant	Pupil absent from school without permission.

Learn the words in the list above, together with their meanings, then answer the questions below.

A   Give one word for each of the following:

1   A pupil who stays away from school without sufficient reason

2   A man who rides his motorbike through a ring of fire

3   A person who is afraid of his own shadow

4   An Arab walking to Mecca, the birthplace of the prophet Mohammed

5   A person who buys things he does not need

B   Complete each sentence with a word from the list.

1   The _____ gloated over his hoard of money.

2   The _____ ate so much at the party that he was sick.

3   The _____ who lived alone in a hut in the forest had not seen anyone for weeks.

4   One of the hunters was captured and eaten by _____ .

5   William Tell was a famous Swiss _____ who loved his country so much that he was prepared to die for it.

Opposites using dis

The opposites of some words are formed by writing **dis** before them.

Examples

appear	**dis**appear
like	**dis**like
honest	**dis**honest
comfort	**dis**comfort

Remember that in writing **dis** before **satisfied** the two letters **s** come together – **dissatisfied**.

A   Write the opposites of these words by placing **dis** before them.

1	agree	9	like
2	allow	10	loyal
3	believe	11	order
4	advantage	12	pleased
5	comfort	13	respect
6	contented	14	satisfied
7	favour	15	taste
8	honest	16	trust

B   Rewrite these sentences, changing the words in bold type so that they will have an opposite meaning.

1   The baby proved to be a very **contented** child.

2   Many people **like** walking.

3   We travelled from London to Brighton in considerable **comfort**.

4   The manager was **satisfied** with the week's takings.

5   The interviewer treated the old man with **respect**.

C   Use one of the words beginning with **dis** to complete each sentence.

1   A cashier who steals money from his employer is _____ .

2   When something is to your _____ it is against your interests.

3   You _____ a person when you think he is telling lies.

4   Things are in _____ when they are not in proper order.

5   People _____ when they hold opposite views on any matter.

disappear

Nouns possession

The sailor used the foot of a rabbit as a charm.

The sailor used a **rabbit's** foot as a charm.

The **'s** in **rabbit's** shows that the foot belonged to a rabbit.

When a plural noun ends with **s** possession is shown by writing the **'** after the **s**.

Examples
ladies' hats
the girls' bicycles

But note:
children's books

Here the noun is plural but it does not end in **s**.

A   Write the missing words.

1   the tail of a kangaroo
    a _____ tail

2   the wool of the sheep
    the _____ wool

3   the ears of a donkey
    a _____ ears

4   the beak of an eagle
    an _____ beak

5   the snout of a pig
    a _____ snout

6   the tail of a lion
    a _____ tail

B   Give the missing words.

1   a school for boys
    a _____ school

2   a nest belonging to robins
    a _____ nest

3   a playground for girls
    a _____ playground

4   a home for dogs
    a _____ home

5   a camp for soldiers
    a _____ camp

6   the trunks belonging to the elephants
    the _____ trunks

7   the tails of the cows
    the _____ tails

8   a meeting for teachers
    a _____ meeting

9   the treasure belonging to the pirates
    the _____ treasure

10 the burrows of the rabbits
    the _____ burrows

C   Use each of these words in a sentence of your own.

cat's	girl's	nurse's
cats'	girls'	nurses'
horse's	boy's	
horses'	boys'	

Pinocchio and the policeman

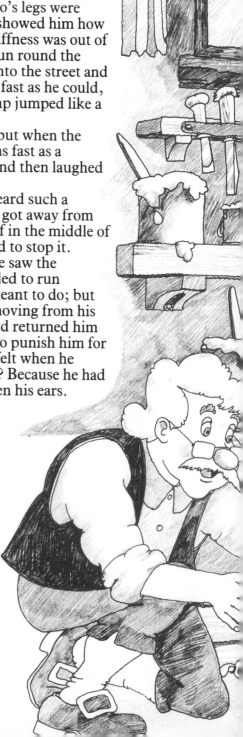

Geppetto took the marionette in his hands and placed him on the floor to see if he could walk; but Pinocchio's legs were stiff. So Geppetto took him by the hand and showed him how to put one foot before the other. When the stiffness was out of his legs Pinocchio began to walk alone, and run round the room; and finally he slipped out of the door into the street and ran away. Poor old Geppetto ran after him as fast as he could, but he could not catch him, for the little scamp jumped like a rabbit.

"Catch him! Catch him!" cried Geppetto; but when the people saw that wooden marionette running as fast as a racehorse they stared at him in amazement, and then laughed and laughed until their sides were sore.

At last a policeman appeared. When he heard such a clatter he thought that somebody's horse had got away from its master; so he courageously planted himself in the middle of the street with his legs wide apart, determined to stop it.

While Pinocchio was still a long way off he saw the policeman barricading the street and he decided to run between his legs before he realized what he meant to do; but he failed dismally. The policeman, without moving from his position, picked him up neatly by the nose and returned him to Geppetto, who meant to pull his ears well to punish him for his naughtiness. Imagine, therefore, how he felt when he couldn't find any ears: and do you know why? Because he had made him in such a hurry that he had forgotten his ears.

The Adventures of Pinocchio   Carlo Collodi

1 Why did Geppetto place the marionette on the floor?
2 Why was Pinocchio unable to walk?
3 How did Geppetto help him to walk?
4 Where did Pinocchio go after learning to walk and run?
5 Why was Geppetto unable to catch him?
6 What did the people do when they saw Pinocchio running?
7 What did the policeman think when he heard such a clatter?
8 What happened to Pinocchio when he tried to run between the policeman's legs?
9 How did Geppetto intend to punish Pinocchio for running away?
10 Why was he unable to carry out this punishment?

Contractions

The short way of writing
has not is **hasn't**.

The short way of writing
you will is **you'll**.

Remember that the apostrophe '
shows that some letters have
been left out when the two words
are joined together.

Now look at these words.

I am	I'm
you are	you're
we are	we're
they are	they're
I have	I've
you have	you've
we have	we've
they have	they've

These shortened words are called
contractions. This is because
they are **contracted** or **made
shorter**.

A   Write a contraction in place of the words in bold
type in these sentences.

1   Thank you, **we have** had a lovely time.

2   I think **I am** getting slimmer.

3   The Joneses say that **they are** going to fly to Italy.

4   Please let me know when **you have** finished your
work.

5   **I have** lost my stamp album.

6   Please tell Susan that **we are** ready to start.

7   We all miss you when **you are** absent from school.

8   Ann and Tom left early as **they have** tickets for the
theatre.

B   Write the contractions for the following.
Some are contained in Books 1 and 2.

1	they are	11	we have
2	it is	12	they will
3	I have	13	you are
4	you will	14	she will
5	I am	15	they have
6	we will	16	is not
7	you have	17	she is
8	he is	18	cannot
9	we are	19	he will
10	I will	20	have not

37

Opposites

above	below
bright	dull
busy	idle
cheap	dear
dead	alive
deep	shallow
drunk	sober
foolish	wise
rough	smooth
tender	tough

A   Write the opposites of these words.
You learnt some of them in Book 2.

1	more	11	deep
2	tender	12	evil
3	quiet	13	dull
4	sharp	14	kind
5	busy	15	alive
6	better	16	awake
7	wise	17	drunk
8	heavy	18	glad
9	wide	19	cheap
10	below	20	rough

B   Rewrite these sentences, changing the words in bold type so as to give them the **opposite** meaning.

Example
1   Food is very **dear** in some parts of Europe.
     Food is very **cheap** in some parts of Europe.

1   Food is very **dear** in some parts of Europe.

2   The cotton mills have been **idle** for many months.

3   The lake was quite **shallow** in places.

4   In only one classroom was the temperature **above** freezing point.

5   The new pupil proved to be a **bright** boy.

6   Our Christmas turkey was very **tough**.

7   The shopkeeper was a very **foolish** man.

8   All the occupants of the boat were **dead**.

9   The police found that the motorist was **sober**.

10   The wood had a **smooth** surface.

Direct speech

"I have a pain in my side," said Eric.

In this sentence the **spoken words** come **first**.

Eric said, **"I have a pain in my side."**

In this sentence the **spoken words** come **last**.

Notice the comma after **said** when the spoken words come last.

A Copy these sentences in your exercise book, putting in speech marks **" "** where required.

1 Sally's mother warned her, Keep away from the fire!

2 The boatman shouted, Any more for the Skylark, please?

3 People in the audience were yelling, More! We want more!

4 Before leaving, Anita said, Thank you for a lovely holiday, Aunt Muriel.

5 Mr. Paul asked, Will you play in goal, Raymond?

B Rewrite these sentences so that the actual words spoken come last.

1 "I can't hear what you say," shouted Peter.

2 "Put your books away, everybody," said the teacher.

3 "My feet are icy cold," muttered the milkman.

4 "Would anyone like another cup of tea?" asked Mrs. Polly.

5 "Is this the way to the hospital?" inquired Richard.

C Rewrite these sentences so that the spoken words come first.

1 The showman shouted, "Three tries for 20p."

2 The old sailor remarked, "There's a big storm blowing up."

3 With a groan the full-back muttered, "I'm afraid my leg is broken."

4 Robin exclaimed, "Thank goodness there are no more exams!"

5 Jennifer's mother whispered, "Hush, David's sleeping."

Compound words

A **compound word** is made up of
two or more words.
tooth+**brush** = **toothbrush**

Examples
cowboy
lighthouse
snowdrop
matchbox

A Write the names of the objects in the pictures,
showing the two words from which each has been
built up.

B In each line join the two words in bold type,
beginning with the second of them.

1 the **light** given by the **sun**

2 **paper** which is stuck on a **wall** of a room

3 the **master** who is **head** of a school

4 the part of a bicycle made to **guard** the
cyclist from **mud**

5 the **pole** to which a **flag** is attached

6 the **stick** to which a **broom** is fastened

7 the **yard** outside a **farm**

8 a **dress** worn by girls and women at **night**

9 a **room** for a **class** of children

10 the **ground** in which children **play**

Young ones

Learn the name of the young of each of these creatures, then answer the questions which follow.

Adult	Young
cat	kitten
cow	calf
deer	fawn
dog	puppy
duck	duckling
eagle	eaglet
goat	kid
hen	chick
lion	cub
sheep	lamb

A   What words are used for:

1   a young dog?
2   a young sheep?
3   a young lion?
4   a young cat?
5   a young goat?
6   a young duck?
7   a young cow?
8   a young hen?
9   a young eagle?
10 a young deer?

B   Write the word which is required to complete each of these sentences.

1   The lioness at the zoo gave birth to two _____.

2   Our spaniel is kept busy looking after her mischievous _____.

3   Betty, the Persian cat, carried one of her _____ in her mouth.

4   The little _____ were sheltering beneath the mother hen's wings.

5   The little _____ followed the mother sheep wherever she went.

6   The nanny-goat and her two _____ were lying down in the field.

7   Followed by her six fluffy yellow _____, the mother duck waddled happily about the farmyard.

8   The eagle dropped the food she had brought right into the open mouths of her _____.

9   The cow mooed loudly for her _____ which had gone astray.

10 In the park we saw a graceful deer and her lovely little _____.

Heidi in the mountains

Heidi was awakened early next morning by a loud whistle. The sun streamed through her little window, and seemed to turn everything in the attic to gold. She looked round, wondering for a moment where she was. Then she heard Alm-Uncle's deep voice outside and knew that she was high up among the mountains.

Quickly she jumped out of bed, dressed, climbed down the ladder and ran out of the hut. There stood Peter with a flock of goats, waiting till Alm-Uncle brought his out of the shed to join them. Heidi ran up to say good-morning to Little Swan and Little Bear.

"Would you like to go with them?" asked her grandfather.

Heidi jumped with joy. "Oh, yes, please."

"You must first wash and make yourself tidy. The sun will laugh at you if you are dirty. See, I have put everything ready for you."

He pointed to a large tub of water. Heidi ran to it and began to splash till her face glowed. Then grandfather went into the hut, and called Peter to bring the wallet.

"Open it," said the old man, and put in a large piece of bread and a lump of cheese. Peter's eyes gleamed, for each was twice the size of the portions he had for his own dinner.

"Now we must put in the little bowl for Heidi to drink from. You must milk two bowlfuls for her when she has her dinner."

Heidi Johanna Spyri

1 How was Heidi awakened early next morning?
2 What did the sun seem to do to everything in the attic?
3 Who was waiting outside the hut?
4 What did he have with him?
5 Why did he stop at the hut?
6 What did Heidi's grandfather tell her to do before going off with the goats?
7 What had he put ready for her to wash herself?
8 What were the names of the grandfather's goats?
9 What did the old man put in the wallet?
10 What would Heidi have to drink with her dinner?

42

Adverbs

Bill walked **slowly** down the lane.

The word **slowly** tells us **how** Bill walked.

He could have walked in several different ways, each of which could be described by one word:

Examples

briskly	leisurely
hurriedly	joyfully

Words which describe how actions are done are called adverbs.

All the adverbs given end with **-ly**, though some adverbs do not.

Example
The doctor did his work **well**.

When **-ly** is added to some words spelling changes are necessary.

Change **y** to **i**

easy	easily
merry	merrily
heavy	heavily
lucky	luckily

Drop **e**

gentle	gently
true	truly
noble	nobly
humble	humbly

For others no change is needed.

proud	proudly
glad	gladly
plain	plainly
quick	quickly
careful	carefully
truthful	truthfully
thankful	thankfully
mental	mentally

A Write the adverb contained in each of these sentences.

1   The farmer told the hiker plainly what he thought of him.

2   Martin slept soundly all night.

3   The gentleman raised his hat politely.

4   Susan waited patiently for the egg to boil.

5   The bus conductor spoke rudely to the old lady.

6   We all laughed heartily at the clowns in the circus.

7   You should always try to speak distinctly.

8   Sally cried bitterly when she broke her new glasses.

B Form adverbs from these adjectives, then use any six of them in sentences of your own.

1	rough	9	mad
2	vain	10	able
3	cosy	11	haughty
4	terrible	12	loud
5	joking	13	hasty
6	equal	14	pitiful
7	noisy	15	sensible
8	single	16	nimble

Joining sentences

I have a friend.
He has six tame rabbits.

two sentences

I have a friend **who** has six tame
rabbits.

one sentence

We found a purse.
It contained money.

two sentences

We found a purse **which**
contained money.

one sentence

Use **who** for **persons** and **which**
for **things**.

or
if
and
but
that
while
before
unless
because
although

A   Use **who** or **which** to join each pair of
sentences.

1   Mr. Dale has two daughters. They are very much
alike.

2   James found the book. Richard had lost it.

3   The police were looking for a man. He had set fire to
a factory.

4   Jane was given a ring. It had belonged to her
grandmother.

5   David and I met a soldier. He had been awarded the
V.C.

6   At the museum we saw a uniform. It had been worn
by Lord Nelson.

7   Mr. and Mrs. Harris adopted the two children. They
had no one to care for them.

8   Androcles approached the lion. It had a thorn in its
paw.

B   Complete each sentence with the correct word,
chosen from the list on the left.

1   She tried the hat on _____ it was too small.

2   The wounded soldier was cheerful _____ he was in
pain.

3   I shall be cross _____ you tell me the truth.

4   He was absent from school _____ he had a bad cold.

5   The collector took Janet's ticket _____ punched it.

6   I will come to see you _____ you go abroad.

7   You may come with me _____ you promise to be
good.

8   The girls watched television _____ their mother went
to the dentist.

9   It was so cold _____ the ponds were frozen.

10   Put some coal on the fire _____ it will soon be out.

Describing things

Adjectives are very important words because they describe people and things, and so help us to get a picture of them in our minds.

This is R. L. Stevenson's description of Long John Silver.

"He was very **tall** and **strong**, with a face as **big** as a ham – **plain** and **pale**, but **intelligent** and **smiling**."

Notice the adjectives used:

tall
strong
big
plain
pale
intelligent
smiling

Look at these examples:

a **low**, **thatched** cottage

a **tall**, **handsome** man

fair, **glossy**, **wavy** hair

A   Use one adjective to describe each of these nouns.

1 a ____ armchair
2 a ____ dress
3 a ____ school
4 a ____ lamb
5 a ____ nose

6 ____ hair
7 a ____ overcoat
8 a ____ temper
9 a ____ smell
10 a ____ sky

B   Copy these ten nouns in your exercise book, then write two suitable adjectives after each.

1 story
2 food
3 sea
4 path
5 tree

6 gipsy
7 weather
8 sailor
9 flower
10 beach

C   Copy these ten adjectives in your exercise book, then write a suitable noun after each.

1 a thrilling
2 a perilous
3 a nimble
4 a wealthy
5 a brave

6 a sturdy
7 a fertile
8 a faint
9 a glossy
10 a loyal

Proverbs

A proverb is a wise saying which has been in use for hundreds of years.

Learn these proverbs and their meanings.

The early bird catches the worm	People who arrive at a place early are likely to be better off than those who come late.
Don't count your chickens before they are hatched	Don't be too confident about possible gains.
Too many cooks spoil the broth	Too many helpers often get in one another's way.
Empty vessels make most noise	Ignorant people usually talk more than wise people.
Make hay while the sun shines	Make the most of your opportunities when they come.
Look before you leap	Think well before taking any serious step.

A   Copy these proverbs, filling in the missing words.

1   Make _____ while the _____ shines.

2   Too many _____ spoil the _____ .

3   Look before you _____ .

4   The _____ bird catches the _____ .

B   Write the proverb which matches each meaning.

1   Think well before taking any serious step.

2   Don't be too confident about possible gains.

3   Ignorant people usually talk more than wise people.

4   Too many helpers often get in one another's way.

Same sound — different meaning

Some words are pronounced like others but are different in spelling and meaning.

beat	to strike; a policeman's round; to win, overcome
beet	a vegetable
cell	a small room
sell	to exchange for money
feat	a skilful deed
feet	plural of foot
bow	to bend low; front of a ship
bough	a branch
hall	a large room; a large building
haul	to pull
need	to be in want of
knead	to work up dough
peal	a long, loud sound
peel	the skin of fruit
ring	to sound a bell; a circle
wring	to squeeze and twist
time	minutes, hours, etc.
thyme	a herb
yoke	wooden frame for oxen; part of a dress
yolk	yellow part of an egg

A Choose the word which will complete each sentence.

1 A crowd saw Sussex ＿＿ Kent by fifty runs.

2 The cook separated the ＿＿ of the egg from the white.

3 There was a merry ＿＿ of bells as the bridal couple left the church.

4 The man bumped his head on a low ＿＿ of a tree.

5 The convict sat in his ＿＿ thinking of his family.

B Use one pair of words from the list on the left to complete each of the sentences below.

1 At sunset they ＿＿ down the Union Jack on the town ＿＿ flagstaff.

2 Bakers ＿＿ not ＿＿ dough by hand today; machines can do the work.

3 Autumn is the ＿＿ to gather ＿＿ from the garden.

4 Wendy took the ＿＿ off her finger before starting to ＿＿ the clothes.

5 Norman walked for two hours for charity with blistered ＿＿ which was a remarkable ＿＿ for a boy of ten.

Doctor Goldsmith's medicine

Oliver Goldsmith, the author, who was sometimes called Dr. Goldsmith because he had studied medicine, gave away so much to the poor that he had little money left for himself.

One day a poor woman called at his house and asked him if he would come to see her husband who was sick and would not eat any food. When Goldsmith called on the family he found that they were very poor because the man had had no work for a considerable time. He discovered that there was no food in the house.

"Come and see me this evening," said Goldsmith to the wife, "and I will let you have some medicine for your husband."

When the woman called that evening Goldsmith gave her a small box which was quite heavy for its size.

"This is the medicine," he exclaimed. "See that it is properly used and it will do your husband the world of good. But please do not open the box until you get home."

"What are the directions for taking it?" asked the woman.

"You will find full directions inside the box," he replied.

Immediately on reaching home the woman sat down beside her husband and opened the box very carefully. It was full of money, on top of which was a slip of paper bearing the words:

"To be taken as often as necessity requires."

Once again Oliver Goldsmith had given away his money to help the poor.

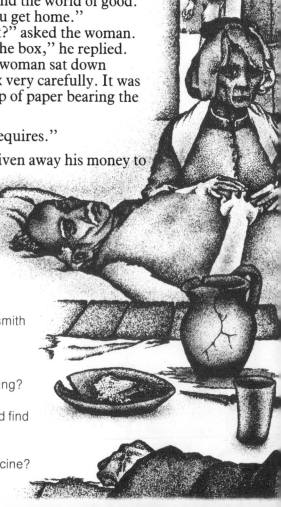

1 Why was Goldsmith sometimes called Doctor although he was really an author?
2 Why did he have little money left for himself?
3 What did the poor woman who called on Goldsmith ask him to do?
4 Why was the woman's family so poor?
5 What did Goldsmith tell the woman to do?
6 What did Goldsmith give the woman that evening?
7 What did Goldsmith ask the woman not to do?
8 Where did Goldsmith tell the woman she would find directions for taking the medicine?
9 What 'medicine' did the box contain?
10 What were the 'directions' given with the medicine?

Direct and indirect speech

"Don't forget your lunch, Alan," said his mother.

Here we have the actual words spoken by Alan's mother **direct** to him. This is called **direct speech** (*see pages 25 and 39*).

If you heard what Alan's mother had said to him, then went out and told someone else, you would probably say:

Alan's mother told him not to forget his lunch.

You would not use her **actual words**.

This is called **indirect speech**.

A   Change these sentences to **indirect speech**.

Examples
"It is time you were in bed, Carol," said her mother. For **direct speech**, speech marks or inverted commas **" "** are needed.

Carol's mother told her it was time she was in bed. For **indirect speech**, speech marks are not needed.

1   "The days are getting longer," remarked Mr. Findlay.

2   "Have you trimmed the hedges, John?" asked Mrs. Gray.

3   "I'm late because of the rain," explained Nigel.

4   "Go on, have another sweet, Michael," urged Fred.

5   "Poke the fire, Alison," said her mother.

6   "Don't go skating on the pond, Colin," warned his father.

B   Change these sentences from **indirect** to **direct speech**.

Example
Charles asked if anybody had seen his exercise book.

"Has anybody seen my exercise book?" asked Charles.

1   Philip told his mother that he was really tired.

2   The landlady remarked that it was a glorious day.

3   Ian told Stephen that he was going to have his dinner.

4   David's teacher told him that she expected better work from him in future.

5   The headmaster announced that he would be leaving at the end of the term.

6   Derek asked Anne if she would like to go to the cinema with him.

Abbreviations

There is a short way of writing some words.

Mr. is short for **Mister**
Rd. is short for **Road**

These shortened forms of words are called **abbreviations**.

a.m.	before noon
B.B.C.	British Broadcasting Corporation
B.R.	British Rail
Co.	Company
D.I.Y.	do it yourself
etc.	and other things
G.P.O.	General Post Office
h.p.	hire-purchase; horse power
k.p.h.	kilometres per hour
No.	Number
p.m.	afternoon
P.C.	Police Constable

A What do these abbreviations stand for?

1 B.R.
2 G.P.O.
3 p.m.
4 h.p.
5 B.B.C.
6 etc.
7 k.p.h.
8 a.m.
9 D.I.Y.
10 Co.
11 P.C.
12 No.

B Give the meaning of the abbreviation in bold type in each sentence.

1 The new cricket bats were supplied by Badger and **Co.**

2 Many cars are bought on the **h.p.** system.

3 The new supermarket has a fine selection of fruit, vegetables, groceries, **etc.**

4 The new play will be televised by the **B.B.C.**

5 The car was travelling at about 80 **k.p.h.**

6 Annette lives in **No.** 8 Church Road.

7 The bank opens at 10 **a.m.**

8 **P.C.** West took down full details of the accident.

9 The train leaves at 4.25 **p.m.**

10 A new **D.I.Y.** store has opened in our town.

Badger and Co.

CRICKET BATS

Using words correctly

whose means **belonging to whom**

who's means **who is**

A

1 Do you know ____ bag this is?

2 I wonder ____ on duty in the library today.

3 The doctor was attending a patient ____ arm was broken.

4 The club leader wants to know ____ responsible for the damage.

5 The woman ____ purse was stolen reported it to the police.

began needs no helping word

begun needs a helping word

B

1 Lessons ____ promptly at nine o'clock.

2 Lessons had ____ when Philip arrived at school.

3 Maureen has ____ to take a pride in her appearance.

4 Work on the new road was ____ yesterday.

5 Workmen ____ work on the new road yesterday.

broke needs no helping word

broken needs a helping word

C

1 A cricket ball ____ the office window.

2 The office window has been ____ several times before.

3 Only two eggs were ____ out of six hundred.

4 A careless packer ____ those two eggs.

5 Andrew admitted that he had ____ the ruler.

6 He ____ it when he hit James with it.

came needs no helping word

come is used with a helping word here

D

1 The dormouse did not venture out till spring had ____.

2 Has the post ____ yet?

3 Yes, it ____ half an hour ago.

4 I hope you will ____ to my party.

5 You ____ to my party last year.

Alphabetical order

Look at these words:

stage
staff
stain
stab
stack

Notice that the first three letters of each word are the same **sta**.

To arrange them in alphabetical order we must look at the **fourth** letter of each.

These are:
g f i b c

Letters in alphabetical order:
b c f g i

Words in alphabetical order:

sta**b**
sta**c**k
sta**f**f
sta**g**e
sta**i**n

Arrange the words in each group in alphabetical order.

A   In these groups look at the **first** letter.

1	handsome	2	linger	3	quiz
	wheel		damage		gloom
	print		bathe		record
	tiger		manage		flour

B   In these groups look at the **second** letter.

4	violet	5	affect	6	luggage
	vulgar		ancient		light
	vowel		abroad		laugh
	vanish		addition		leave
	vestry		active		loyal

C   In these groups look at the **third** letter.

7	blink	8	chilly	9	splash
	blunder		church		spice
	bleak		change		sponge
	blank		chorus		spend
	block		cheat		spring

D   Arrange each group in alphabetical order.

1	heave	2	clever	3	drug
	heath		clergy		drum
	head		clench		drunk
	health		clean		drudge

4	parent	5	brawn	6	strong
	part		bramble		struck
	park		bracket		street
	parcel		branch		stripe

7	recruit	8	when	9	exclaim
	recall		whether		exchange
	recent		where		excess
	recipe		wheel		excite

Similars

abandon	leave
abundant	plentiful
assist	help
cautious	careful
celebrated	famous
centre	middle
conceal	hide
enormous	huge
fortunate	lucky
insolent	cheeky
obstinate	stubborn
pathetic	pitiful
reckless	rash
slender	slim
squander	waste
sufficient	enough
summit	top
vacant	empty
vanish	disappear
wealthy	rich

A   Copy these sentences, using a simpler word for each word in bold type.

1   Sir David is a **wealthy** banker.

2   I will **assist** you in the shop.

3   The house has been **vacant** for months.

4   He was **fortunate** to escape with slight injuries.

5   Simon did his best to **conceal** the ball he had stolen.

6   When we reached the **summit** of the mountain we rested.

7   There was an **enormous** swelling on the boxer's forehead.

8   The garage was in the **centre** of the town.

9   Apples are **abundant** in the autumn.

10   There was **sufficient** petrol in the car for a long run.

B   In each group below select the word which is similar in meaning to the word in bold type.

1 **squander**	2 **cautious**	3 **obstinate**
roam	willing	tender
wander	serious	stubborn
waste	sad	proud
hoard	careful	cruel

4 **abandon**	5 **vanish**	6 **celebrated**
leave	conquer	wealthy
gather	disappear	handsome
search	paint	muscular
renew	scatter	famous

7 **pathetic**	8 **reckless**	9 **slender**
aged	careful	stout
honoured	clever	slim
dishonest	rash	tender
pitiful	timid	flabby

Michael at the clinic

Michael followed his mother into the clinic, where a red-haired nurse took his name. She remarked that Doctor would probably discharge him today. Michael's scowl returned. "Hope he doesn't," he muttered. The nurse left him scuffing his shoes against the bar of a chair in the waiting room.

Presently his turn came to go into the surgery. Another nurse took off his jacket. A white-coated doctor felt his left arm. He made him turn his wrist from side to side. "Now waggle your fingers and thumb," he said, gripping Michael's arm. It did not hurt at all, but Michael managed a convincing "Oow!" and pulled his arm away.

Doctor was not taken in. He smiled at Mother. "Last week's X-rays shows that the cracked bone has healed perfectly," he said. "Your boy won't have any more trouble with it, Mrs. Blake." He took Michael's jacket from Nurse and helped him into it. "Let me see," he said pleasantly, "this is Whit week half-term. School reopens on Monday. Back you go, young man. You must be careful of your arm at first. Otherwise you're as fit as a fiddle."

Michael and the Music Makers   Harry Fleming

1 Who took Michael's name at the clinic?
2 What remark did this person make?
3 What effect did this remark have on Michael?
4 What was Michael doing when the nurse left him?
5 What did the doctor make Michael do with his wrist?
6 What did the doctor tell Michael to do when he gripped his arm?
7 What had been the matter with Michael's arm?
8 How did the doctor know that Michael's arm had healed perfectly?
9 When did Michael have to go back to school?
10 What did the doctor tell Michael to do at first when he returned to school?

Occupations

bank clerk
bookseller
bricklayer
cameraman
cashier
decorator
fishmonger
model

newsagent
potter
reporter
salesman
shepherd
umpire
veterinary surgeon

A Write the names of these occupations.

B Write the missing occupations.

1 It took the ____ ten days to build the garden wall.

2 A detailed account of the accident was written by the ____ of the local paper.

3 I asked the ____ for a statement of my account.

4 This vase was made by our local ____ .

5 The ____ reduced the prices of the gardening books.

6 Patrick handed the bill and the money to the ____ at the café.

7 We hope the ____ will finish papering and painting the lounge by next Saturday.

8 A ____ was trying to sell Mrs. Grey a washing machine.

9 The ____ was displaying the latest fashion in summer dresses.

10 The ____ raised his hand to show that the batsman was out.

C What name is given to the person who:

1 looks after sheep?

2 rides horses in races?

3 sells newspapers and magazines?

Prepositions

off   before
behind   in
across   on
under   over
into   near

Use the words in the list on the left to fill the spaces in the sentences below.

1   Humpty fell _____ the wall.

2   The man dived _____ the pool.

3   The horse jumped _____ the fence.

4   The dog is _____ the table.

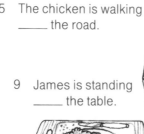

5   The chicken is walking _____ the road.

6   There is an apple _____ the dish.

7   There are flowers _____ the vase.

8   There is a guard _____ the fire.

9   James is standing _____ the table.

10   John is hiding _____ the armchair.

56

Forming nouns from verbs

Verb	Noun
act	action
allow	allowance
arrive	arrival
behave	behaviour
defend	defence
defy	defiance
deliver	delivery
discover	discovery
enter	entrance
grow	growth
hate	hatred
injure	injury
invite	invitation
know	knowledge
marry	marriage
obey	obedience
press	pressure
produce	production
remain	remainder
succeed	success

A   Write the missing nouns formed from the verbs in bold type.

1   a generous ____   **allow**
2   a strong ____   **defend**
3   prompt ____   **deliver**
4   a painful ____   **injure**
5   a hasty ____   **act**
6   a wide ____   **enter**
7   a happy ____   **marry**
8   a British ____   **produce**
9   great ____   **press**
10 a huge ____   **succeed**

B   Write the noun, formed from the verb in bold type, which will complete each sentence.

1   The children's ____ at the pantomime was excellent.   **behave**

2   The dog gobbled up the ____ of the turkey.   **remain**

3   Bruce read about the ____ of America by Christopher Columbus.   **discover**

4   We watched the ____ of the plant with interest.   **grow**

5   June sent Judith an ____ to her birthday party.   **invite**

6   The teacher expected ____ from all her pupils.   **obey**

7   Crowds watched the ____ of Santa Claus in his lovely scarlet robe.   **arrive**

8   The patient went out in ____ of his doctor's orders.   **defy**

9   "____ is power" is a well-known saying.   **know**

Verbs past tense and participle

Present tense	Past tense	Participle
buy	bought	bought
kneel	knelt	knelt
mow	mowed	mown
saw	sawed	sawn
sew	sewed	sewn
spring	sprang	sprung
swear	swore	sworn
swell	swelled	swollen
tread	trod	trodden
wind	wound	wound

Remember that a participle always needs a helping word.

Example
The patient's arm **had swollen** during the night.

The word **had** helps the participle **swollen**.

Many vintage cars and motorcycles **have been bought** by the museum.

The words **have been** help the participle **bought**.

Write the form of the verb in bold type, **past tense** or **participle**, which will fill each space.

1 Kevin _____ the alarm clock this evening. **wind**

2 The woodman rested when he had _____ all the wood. **saw**

3 Janet _____ the skirt by hand. **sew**

4 The gardener _____ both lawns yesterday. **mow**

5 Helen feared that her kitten would be _____ on. **tread**

6 These gloves were _____ by hand. **sew**

7 Christopher _____ to say his prayers. **kneel**

8 The old boat had _____ a leak and was sinking. **spring**

9 The tiger _____ at the daring hunter. **spring**

10 Both of the scouts had been _____ to secrecy. **swear**

11 The river was _____ by the torrential rain. **swell**

12 Mrs. Boyce _____ a winter coat in the sale. **buy**

Fun with words

A   In each group below, the second word of each pair is formed by writing a letter **after** the first word. A different letter is used for each group. Look at the letter that is added and write the missing words.

Example

bar	bare		bar	bar**e**
fin	fine		fin	fin**e**
hop	____		hop	hop**e**

In this group the letter **e** is added.

1	rip	ripe	2	tea	team	3	pin	pink
	ton	tone		war	warm		for	fork
	wag	____		fir	____		bun	____

4	for	fort	5	bat	bath	6	ban	band
	ten	tent		was	wash		her	herd
	hear	____		clot	____		grin	____

7	sea	seal	8	bee	beer	9	win	wing
	knee	kneel		pea	pear		ran	rang
	ear	____		boa	____		son	____

B   In each group the second word is formed by changing one of the letters of the first word. Find the letter to be changed in each group, then write the missing words.

Example

harp	hard		har**p**	har**d**
slip	slid		sli**p**	sli**d**
steep	____		stee**p**	stee**d**

In this group the letter **p** is changed to **d**.

1	bard	bird	2	mix	six	3	bald	bale
	farm	firm		mail	sail		ward	ware
	grand	____		mole	____		find	____

4	part	port	5	lone	long	6	bore	sore
	last	lost		pane	pang		bend	send
	came	____		thine	____		blink	____

7	shot	spot	8	bone	bore	9	hung	lung
	shin	spin		mane	mare		heap	leap
	shade	____		bind	____		harder	____

Sir Henry springs a visit

Time and again Ben returned to the Spanish Steps. They were near the hotel, ideal for spare hours when he dared not be absent too long. His favourite place was at the very top, with the street and church behind him and the western skyline, with the Vatican and the long Janiculum ridge, stretched out in front.

There was always so much life and movement there. People streamed up and down like the angels on Jacob's Ladder, endlessly. There were a hundred and thirty-seven steps. He had counted them. If he saw an interesting character toiling up, he could rely on that person pausing for a few minutes at the top. There was usually time for at least a lightning sketch.

Frankly, too, as he had heard men say in Covent Garden Market, it was a good pitch. He sold several sketches there.

He would have sold another – but for Sir Henry. An interested German tourist was already hovering at his elbow, but the drawing was fated to remain in the book, with Ben's methodical note, "Unfinished Flower Girl, Rome, Feb. 14, 1815." Suddenly Sir Henry exploded behind them.

"You young devil! So it's true!"

Ben sprang to his feet and turned. Sir Henry was just dismounting from Lord Frederick's crested carriage, which had pulled up in front of the church door. Lord Frederick and Sir Rupert Dodds were watching amusedly.

"I beg your pardon, sir. You were requiring me?"

"I was told I'd likely find you here. Gad, a servant of mine! Hawking goods in the street like a cheapjack! My friends will be asking, don't I pay you enough?"

Violet for Bonaparte   Geoffrey Trease

1 In which year is this story set?
2 In which country does the incident take place?
3 For what reason did Ben choose to work at the Spanish Steps?
4 What could Ben see from his favourite place at the top?
5 What made the Steps an ideal place for an artist to work?
6 What do you think is meant by a 'lightning sketch'?
7 Ben had previously lived in another city. Can you tell which?
8 What occupation had Ben besides being an artist?
9 Which sketch had the tourist been about to buy?
10 Why was Sir Henry's anger so great at finding Ben there?

The doers of actions

The names of doers of actions can often be formed by adding **-er** to a verb or a noun.

teach	teacher
read	reader
jump	jumper

If the verb ends with **e** this letter is dropped when adding **-er**.

bake	baker
write	writer
use	user

Some words double the last letter when **-er** is added.

run	runner
rob	robber
swim	swimmer

When the verb ends with **y** (but not ay, ey or oy) the **y** is changed to **i** before **-er** is added.

fly	flier
cry	crier
carry	carrier

A　What is the word for:

1　one who bowls?

2　one who sings?

3　one who weaves?

4　one who builds?

5　one who drums?

6　one who boxes?

7　one who grumbles?

8　one who wins?

9　one who explores?

10　one who settles?

B　Write the word needed to fill each space. Look at the words in bold type at the end of each line.

1　The ___ knocked him out with a straight right on the jaw.　**box**

2　One ___ was a long way behind the main party.　**straggle**

3　Crowds watched the ___ descend the ladder into the sea.　**dive**

4　Every ___ received a free sample of coffee.　**shop**

5　These peas were grown by our ___.　**garden**

6　The little ___ made his way along the path.　**toddle**

7　Alan has never won a race but he is a determined ___.　**run**

8　The ___ lost hundreds of pounds at the races.　**gamble**

9　The acrobat is a brilliant ___.　**perform**

10　One ___ was arrested by the police.　**strike**

Adjectives

A   Copy the adjectives in column **a** in your book, then write after each adjective the noun in column **b** which matches it.

a	b
mountainous	flower
scorching	pupil
deafening	tiger
shabby	mother
fragrant	voice
gigantic	heat
intelligent	clothes
hoarse	country
ferocious	shout
devoted	strength

B   Fit the adjectives in the list on the left into their correct places in the sentences below.

deadly
rugged
fragile
tarnished
boundless
wholesome
celebrated
forbidding
strenuous
frequent

1   To be healthy we must eat ___ food.

2   Hurricanes are ___ here in autumn.

3   Some plants contain a ___ poison.

4   Cornwall has a very ___ coastline.

5   We did some ___ exercises to try and lose weight.

6   A large audience heard the recital by the ___ pianist.

7   Securely packed in a box of straw was a ___ china ornament.

8   They were cleaning the ___ silver.

9   The girl's face fell when she saw the ___ look on the face of her teacher.

10   The inventor was a man of ___ energy.

C   Use these adjectives in sentences of your own, one sentence for each adjective.

gorgeous	insolent
obstinate	hideous
efficient	accurate
colossal	candid

Punctuation

Putting full stops, commas, question marks, etc., in sentences is called **punctuation**.

A full stop is used to end a sentence which makes a statement.

Example
Gold is mined in South Africa.

A question mark is used to end a sentence which asks a question.

Example
How many days are there in a week?

Commas are used:

to separate the name of a person directly spoken to from the rest of the sentence.

Examples
Richard, have you locked the door?
Have you locked the door, Richard?

to separate words in a sentence when **and** or **or** is used to separate the last two words only.

Example
Gold, iron, silver and lead are all metals.

after words like **well**, **oh**, **yes**, **no** and **now** when they begin a sentence.

Example
Well, I warned you not to do it.

to set off the word **please** at the end of a sentence.

Example
Have you the right time, please?

An exclamation mark ! is used after a word or a sentence which is spoken excitedly.

Example
Run! The tide's coming in fast!

Insert punctuation marks in these sentences.

1   Have you ever spent a holiday abroad

2   Yes I went to Spain last summer

3   Hold tight the brakes are not working

4   Now where was I before I was interrupted

5   Please lock up before you go Philip

6   Oh look at that dear little rabbit

7   Jennifer have you finished your homework

8   Cyprus Corsica Malta Elba and Sicily are all islands

Rhymes

A   In the list on the left are six pairs of rhyming words.
Fit them into their correct places in the verses below.

hills
mills

miles
isles

curled
world

flow
go

breast
dressed

tree
me

Great, wide, beautiful, wonderful ____, 1
With the wonderful water round you ____, 2
And the wonderful grass upon your ____ 3
World, you are beautifully ____. 4

The wonderful air is over ____, 5
And the wonderful wind is shaking the ____, 6
It walks on the water, and whirls the ____, 7
And talks to itself on the tops of the ____. 8

You friendly earth! how far do you ____, 9
With the wheat-fields that nod, and the rivers that ____, 10
With cities and gardens, and cliffs and ____ 11
And people upon you for thousands of ____? 12

B   Write the words which will complete these sentences. Each word rhymes with the word in bold type in the same line.

Example   1 **please**   missing word is **freeze**

1 In winter the ponds and rivers sometimes ____. **please**

2 A police car soon arrived on the ____ of the accident. **queen**

3 Instead of improving his writing gets ____. **purse**

4 The robins ate every ____ of bread. **slum**

5 The duchess wore a long velvet ____. **poke**

6 In spring the farmers ____ their fields. **cow**

C   Write the following as six lines of poetry.

In the dark and lonely night, when the stars are all alight, sleep comes creeping up the street with her naked silent feet carrying upon her back dreams of all kinds in a sack.

Words with more than one meaning

Some words have more than one meaning.

The miser was too **mean** to buy himself food.

Some words **mean** much the same as other words.

check
hiding
lock
score
sound
spoke
stamp
stone
swallow
train

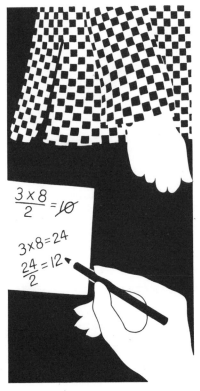

A   Use the words in the list on the left to fill the spaces below. The same word must be used for each pair of sentences.

1   You should ____ the working of every sum.
    Farmer Brown wore a ____ suit.

2   In very cold weather workmen ____ their feet to get warm.
    I put a ____ on the letter and posted it.

3   The ____ arrived at the station an hour late.
    Footballers ____ hard to keep fit.

4   It was quiet; not a ____ was to be heard.
    One apple was damaged; the rest were _____ .

5   Pam's plum had a huge ____ in it.
    A big ____ had broken the classroom window.

6   The two boys were ____ behind the oak tree.
    His father gave him a good ____ for robbing birds' nests.

7   A ____ had built its nest under the eaves.
    His throat was so sore that he could hardly _____ .

8   A forward's job is to ____ goals for his side.
    There are twenty in a _____ .

9   When people go out they should ____ their doors.
    There were two boats in the canal _____ .

10 Nobody ____ a word during the music.
    There is a bent ____ in the front wheel of Roger's bicycle.

B   Write ten sentences of your own showing how each of these words can have two different meanings.

can   right   trunk

litter   light

Lucy comes to Hagworthy

Stepping out onto the platform, Lucy looked around expectantly. Two other people got off the train, but apart from the porter there was no-one else to be seen. She picked up the suitcases and began to walk towards the ticket office with a sudden sinking feeling. Surely her father hadn't made a muddle over the day? And then a remembered figure appeared at the flight of steps leading up from the little car park below the station – Aunt Mabel, in the same hairy suit that she had said goodbye in five years ago, peering round short-sightedly, heaving a little as she got her breath back after the climb.

They kissed, awkwardly. The porter took Lucy's cases and produced a crate of bottles and a parcel. Could Miss Clough kindly drop them off at Hagworthy?

The crate and the suitcases quite filled the back of Aunt Mabel's small car. Lucy got into the front seat: obviously there would have been no room for Kester and the girls. No doubt that was why they hadn't come. She glanced sideways at Aunt Mabel, who was hunting for the car keys in a handbag that was a turmoil of gloves, handkerchiefs and pieces of paper. She seemed quite undisturbed by their loss, and she had said none of the conventional things about how Lucy had grown, had she had a good journey, and how was her father. She had simply absorbed her niece, along with the crate and the parcel.

The Wild Hunt of Hagworthy   Penelope Lively

1   How many people got off the train?
2   Why did Lucy have a 'sudden sinking feeling'?
3   How was the car park reached from the station?
4   How long was it since Lucy had seen Aunt Mabel?
5   What physical defect did Aunt Mabel have?
6   Which words tell you that she was probably plump?
7   Why do you think Lucy and Aunt Mabel felt awkward when they kissed?
8   What was Aunt Mabel's full name?
9   Explain what you think is meant by the last sentence in the extract.
10 What impression from this extract do you get of Aunt Mabel as a person?

Opposites

coward	hero
few	many
first	last
float	sink
forget	remember
found	lost
friend	enemy; foe
loose	tight
narrow	wide; broad
often	seldom

A   Write the opposites of these words. Some you will remember from exercise 38.

1	lost	11	often
2	smooth	12	dead
3	friend	13	remember
4	deep	14	cheap
5	few	15	wide
6	below	16	wise
7	last	17	float
8	tough	18	drunk
9	tight	19	hero
10	busy	20	bright

B   Write the missing words, which are the opposites of the words in bold type.

1   We watched the tin **float** for some time, then it began to ____ .

2   In battle the soldier who was thought to be a **coward** proved himself a ____ .

3   He has hundreds of **friends** and no ____ .

4   The trousers were too **tight** in the legs and too ____ in the waist.

5   James is usually **first** up and ____ to go to bed.

6   The ring which was **lost** in the morning was ____ in the afternoon.

7   The river was very **narrow** at its source but very ____ at its mouth.

8   Robert **remembered** to post his father's letter but ____ to stick a stamp on the envelope.

9   Jean ____ visits us, but we **seldom** see Sandra.

10   **Many** people seek fame, but ____ find it.

Subject and predicate

A sentence has two parts, **subject** and **predicate**.

Subject
This is the person or thing spoken about.

Predicate
This is what is said about the subject.

Subject	Predicate
The little girl	kissed her mother.
The tired boy	sat down on the grass.
Sheep	bleat.

A   Divide these sentences into **subject** and **predicate**.

1   A bank of cloud covered the sun.

2   Our new teacher has wavy brown hair.

3   The whole family goes to church on Sundays.

4   The two chimpanzees escaped from the zoo.

5   The rough seas capsized the little boat.

B   Pair these **subjects** and **predicates**.

1   The stationmaster   in bad weather.

2   Meat and vegetables   walked on his hind legs.

3   The plane took off   is said to be haunted.

4   The clever dog   explained why the train was late.

5   The lonely cottage   make a satisfying meal.

C   Add a suitable **predicate** to these **subjects**.

1   The busy shopkeeper ....

2   A juicy apple ....

3   The racing car ....

4   The roar of a lion ....

5   A bunch of flowers ....

D   Write a suitable **subject** before each of these **predicates**.

1   .... had to retire from the race.

2   .... was taken to the police station.

3   .... rowed back to the ship.

4   .... make children very happy.

5   .... spilt milk on the carpet.

68

Agreement of subject and verb

The subject of a sentence must agree with its verb.

A **singular subject** requires a **singular verb**.

Example
The **boy plays** football every Saturday.

A **plural subject** requires a **plural verb**.

Example
The **boys play** football every Saturday.

Always use a **singular verb** with these words:
each, anybody, nobody, everybody, everyone, no one, either, neither

Examples
Neither of the two boys **was** to blame.
Nobody likes having to admit a mistake.

Use a **plural verb** when two singular nouns in the subject are joined by **and**.

Example
The dog **and** the cat **are** quite friendly.

Singular	Plural
does	do
cleans	clean
goes	go
has	have
is	are
makes	make
takes	take
says	say
puts	put
was	were

Choose the correct verb from the pair above to complete each sentence.

1 **make   makes**
   The cook ____ delicious queen cakes.

2 **clean   cleans**
   She ____ her car regularly.

3 **has   have**
   Everybody ____ to eat in order to live.

4 **do   does**
   She ____ her best to improve her spelling.

5 **put   puts**
   Tony and Paul always ____ their toys away.

6 **make   makes**
   The children ____ a noise when they play.

7 **take   takes**
   Some people ____ their pets on holiday.

8 **is   are**
   Neither of these two books ____ suitable.

9 **do   does**
   Some pupils ____ their best to write neatly.

Words to complete words

A   A word of four letters is needed to complete each of the unfinished words in these sentences. Make a list of these four-letter words.

Example   1 **card** **card**igan

1   This woollen _ _ _ _igan will keep you warm.

2   He scored a _ _ _ _ury in his very first innings.

3   I have come to the last _ _ _ _ter in my book.

4   Roger and his _ _ _ _ner gave a fine exhibition of dancing.

5   The _ _ _ _oon burst when Tony was blowing it up.

6   The _ _ _ _ory manufactures a large variety of toys.

7   It did not take the nurse long to _ _ _ _age the patient's leg.

8   We will start work in _ _ _ _est next Monday morning.

B   This exercise is similar to **A** but the missing words come at the end of the unfinished words.

Example   1 **mark** re**mark**

1   A spectator passed a rude re_ _ _ _ about the referee.

2   The cowboy put a br_ _ _ _ on his horse.

3   He got the boat at the bar_ _ _ _ price of £250.

4   A re_ _ _ _ of £50 was offered for the return of the lost watch.

5   The parents would not give their con_ _ _ _ to the marriage.

6   The class had to trans_ _ _ _ a French story into English.

7   Strong pillars were needed to sup_ _ _ _ the heavy platform.

8   Pat had an ob_ _ _ _ sheet of cardboard ten centimetres long and six centimetres wide.

9   The prisoner made his es_ _ _ _ by climbing over the prison wall.

Same sound — different meaning

Learn the spelling and the meaning of each word in the list before attempting the exercise.

die — to stop living
dye — to colour or stain

four — one more than three
fore — at the front

pray — to ask God
prey — animal hunted for food

rain — water from the clouds
reign — act of ruling
rein — strap which guides a horse

seam — a join in cloth
seem — to appear to be

right — opposite of left; correct
write — to form words on a surface

stair — a step
stare — to look with wide eyes

steal — to take another's property
steel — a very hard metal

wait — to stay or pause
weight — how heavy a thing is

waist — part of the body
waste — to make poor use of

A Use the words in the list on the left to complete these sentences.

1 A horse has ____ legs; two hind legs and two ____ legs.

2 These knives and forks are made of stainless ____.

3 The Second World War broke out in the ____ of George VI.

4 Jenny decided to ____ her red dress black.

5 Two pieces of material can be joined by making a ____.

6 You will ____ a lot of material if you make the dress too slack in the ____.

7 Thousands of people ____ for the peace of the world.

8 Most people ____ with their ____ hand.

9 The film star stopped on the top ____ to ____ at the crowd.

B Write the words which are pronounced like those below but which have a different spelling and meaning.

1 sell
2 ball
3 need
4 leak
5 beat
6 peel
7 great
8 feet
9 fur
10 bow
11 ring
12 hall
13 hole
14 time
15 been
16 flower
17 him
18 yolk
19 peace
20 male

International airport

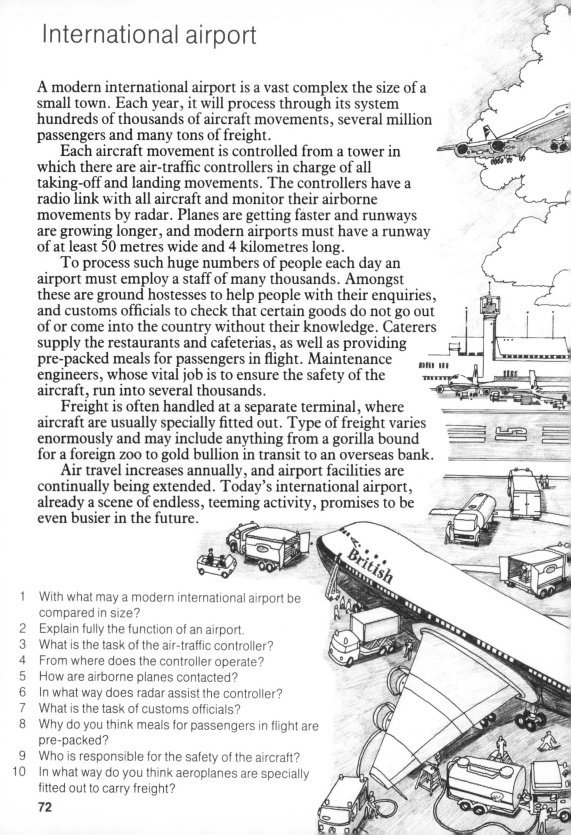

A modern international airport is a vast complex the size of a small town. Each year, it will process through its system hundreds of thousands of aircraft movements, several million passengers and many tons of freight.

Each aircraft movement is controlled from a tower in which there are air-traffic controllers in charge of all taking-off and landing movements. The controllers have a radio link with all aircraft and monitor their airborne movements by radar. Planes are getting faster and runways are growing longer, and modern airports must have a runway of at least 50 metres wide and 4 kilometres long.

To process such huge numbers of people each day an airport must employ a staff of many thousands. Amongst these are ground hostesses to help people with their enquiries, and customs officials to check that certain goods do not go out of or come into the country without their knowledge. Caterers supply the restaurants and cafeterias, as well as providing pre-packed meals for passengers in flight. Maintenance engineers, whose vital job is to ensure the safety of the aircraft, run into several thousands.

Freight is often handled at a separate terminal, where aircraft are usually specially fitted out. Type of freight varies enormously and may include anything from a gorilla bound for a foreign zoo to gold bullion in transit to an overseas bank.

Air travel increases annually, and airport facilities are continually being extended. Today's international airport, already a scene of endless, teeming activity, promises to be even busier in the future.

1 With what may a modern international airport be compared in size?
2 Explain fully the function of an airport.
3 What is the task of the air-traffic controller?
4 From where does the controller operate?
5 How are airborne planes contacted?
6 In what way does radar assist the controller?
7 What is the task of customs officials?
8 Why do you think meals for passengers in flight are pre-packed?
9 Who is responsible for the safety of the aircraft?
10 In what way do you think aeroplanes are specially fitted out to carry freight?

Common sayings

Our language contains thousands of common sayings not found in other languages. It is important to know them and to understand them, for at first sight many of them do not make sense.

Example
to let the cat out of the bag means to give away a secret

Common saying	Meaning
to hit below the belt	to act unfairly towards an opponent
to have a bone to pick with someone	to have a dispute to settle or a complaint to make
to paddle one's own canoe	to do things for oneself
to put the cart before the horse	to do things the wrong way round
to let the cat out of the bag	to give away a secret
to make both ends meet	to live within one's means
to have a feather in one's cap	to have done something to be proud of
to hang one's head	to be ashamed of oneself
to turn over a new leaf	to lead a new life
to get into hot water	to get into trouble

Complete these sayings and give the meaning of each.

1 to let the ____ out of the ____

2 to get into ____ water

3 to make both ____ meet

4 to paddle one's own ____

5 to have a ____ in one's cap

6 to hit below the ____

7 to ____ one's head

8 to have a ____ to ____ with someone

9 to turn over a new ____

10 to put the ____ before the ____

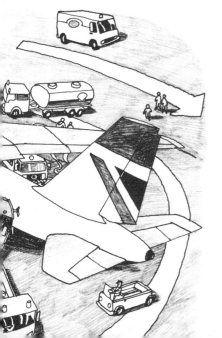

Similars

annual	yearly
attempt	try
cease	stop
circular	round
coarse	rough
courageous	brave
drowsy	sleepy
generous	kind
inquire	ask
insane	mad
manufacture	make
moist	damp
necessity	need
portion	part
purchase	buy
putrid	rotten
rare	scarce
regret	sorrow
reply	answer
scared	frightened

A Copy the words in column **a**, then opposite each write the word in column **b** which is similar in meaning.

a	b
inquire	stop
necessity	rotten
rare	damp
circular	need
drowsy	sorrow
moist	round
cease	ask
putrid	part
regret	scarce
portion	sleepy

B In place of each word in bold type write a simpler word which has a similar meaning.

1 Sir Malcolm was thanked for his **generous** gift to the hospital.

2 There will be a big crowd to see the champion driver **attempt** to break the world record next month.

3 I have received no **reply** to my letter.

4 After his huge Sunday lunch Tim felt quite **drowsy**.

5 The material is very **coarse**.

6 People **purchase** warm clothing in readiness for winter.

7 The **annual** Flower Show is held in September.

8 Anne was **scared** of the big bloodhound.

9 The murderer was found guilty but **insane**.

10 Captain Smith was decorated for his **courageous** deed.

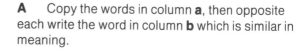

Words which save work

One word can sometimes do the work of several.

Example
At the end of the week Adrian was **without a penny**.

At the end of the week Adrian was **penniless**.

annually
bareheaded
briefly
capsized
correctly
decide
died
disappeared
homeless
improving
mad; insane
miser
rescued
returned
soon
suddenly
useless
widow

A   Use one word in place of those in bold type in each sentence. All the labour-saving words are in the list on the left.

1   The boarding-house was kept by a **woman whose husband was dead**.

2   The lifeboat **saved the lives of** the crew of the sinking ship.

3   The old man **passed away** in his sleep.

4   The manager went to London but **came back again** next day.

5   As a result of the fire several people were **without a home**.

6   I hope to see you **before very long**.

7   Cyril was **of no use** in the garden.

8   The shipwrecked sailor was **out of his mind**.

9   The pickpocket soon **went out of sight**.

10 Mary's writing is **getting better** every day.

B

1   The reporter told his story **in very few words**.

2   Keith could not **make up his mind** which book to buy.

3   Peter worked ten sums **without making a single mistake**.

4   The Welsh National Eisteddfod is held **once every year**.

5   **Without any warning** a policeman appeared on the scene.

6   Nobody admires a **man who hoards his money**.

7   The boys went to school **with nothing on their heads**.

8   The little boat **turned completely upside down**.

Twin words

Many expressions consist of two simple words joined by the word **and**.

Learn the expressions in the list, then answer the questions which follow.

cats and dogs
down and out
fair and square
far and wide
fits and starts
give and take
hammer and tongs
hand and foot
head and shoulders
lock and key
safe and sound
slow and sure

A Write the missing words.

1 give and ____
2 fits and ____
3 slow and ____
4 head and ____
5 down and ____
6 safe and ____
7 ____ and key
8 ____ and square
9 ____ and foot
10 ____ and tongs
11 ____ and dogs
12 ____ and wide

B Write the missing word in each sentence. Learn how each expression is used.

1 The two men were fighting hammer and ____ .

2 My mother keeps the sweets under lock and ____ .

3 Robin is ____ and shoulders above the other boys.

4 The police searched far and ____ for the missing girl.

5 The prisoner was bound hand and ____ .

6 The poor traveller looked ____ and out.

7 The bully was beaten fair and ____ by a smaller boy.

8 People should learn to ____ and take in life.

9 It was raining cats and ____ so the children stayed indoors.

10 After a long and perilous journey the explorers arrived back ____ and sound.

C Write six sentences of your own, each containing one of the expressions in your list.

Noises of creatures

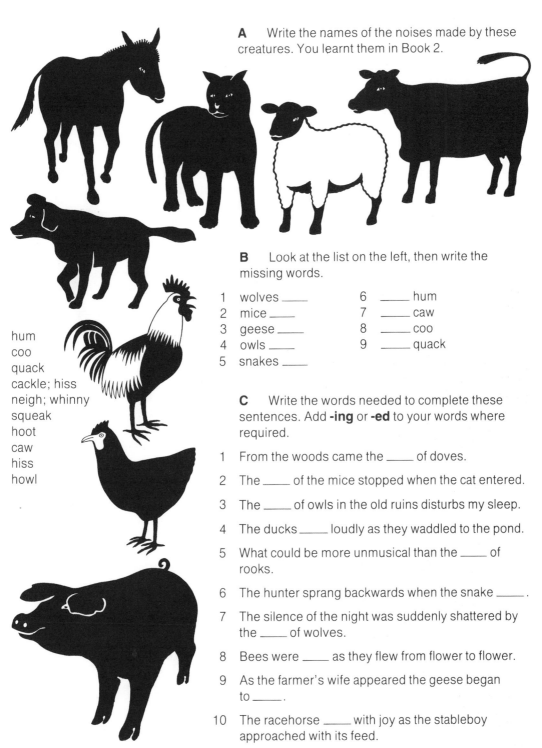

A Write the names of the noises made by these creatures. You learnt them in Book 2.

hum
coo
quack
cackle; hiss
neigh; whinny
squeak
hoot
caw
hiss
howl

B Look at the list on the left, then write the missing words.

1 wolves ____
2 mice ____
3 geese ____
4 owls ____
5 snakes ____

6 ____ hum
7 ____ caw
8 ____ coo
9 ____ quack

C Write the words needed to complete these sentences. Add **-ing** or **-ed** to your words where required.

1 From the woods came the ____ of doves.

2 The ____ of the mice stopped when the cat entered.

3 The ____ of owls in the old ruins disturbs my sleep.

4 The ducks ____ loudly as they waddled to the pond.

5 What could be more unmusical than the ____ of rooks.

6 The hunter sprang backwards when the snake ____.

7 The silence of the night was suddenly shattered by the ____ of wolves.

8 Bees were ____ as they flew from flower to flower.

9 As the farmer's wife appeared the geese began to ____.

10 The racehorse ____ with joy as the stableboy approached with its feed.

Rocky and the lioness

Rocky swung round and looked at the scrub. His heart thumped out of time. A lioness had just come out of the scrub. It was watching him with its wicked, intelligent eyes. Rocky grabbed his rifle. The lioness began to walk towards him on stiff legs. It was about fifty metres away. Its tail twitched and it began to walk more quickly.

Rocky brought the rifle to his shoulder and looked along the sights. He couldn't see the animal's chest because its head was down, so he aimed at a spot between its eyes and squeezed the trigger. He felt the kick of the rifle against his shoulder, felt the blast of the explosion, and saw the spurt of dust behind the lioness where his bullet had hit the ground. He had missed, and the lioness growled, its tail lashed, and it charged. Its speed was tremendous. It bounded silently at him, and Rocky could see its flat, evil head, its big teeth and long, tearing claws. He rattled the bolt of his rifle. It jammed, and he started to sweat.

And then, ten metres from him, the lioness twisted in the air and fell. There was a long spear sticking out of its shoulder. It snarled and bit at the shaft, snarled again, reared up and fell backwards, dead.

Rocky stared at the dead lioness for a few seconds. He wiped his face and nodded to Kukulu.

"Thanks, Kukulu," he said quietly. "It's a good thing that you're a better shot with your spear than I am with my rifle."

Rocky and the Lions   R. B. Maddock

1   Where had the lioness come from?
2   What effect did its appearance have on Rocky's heart?
3   Write the two adjectives used to describe the eyes of the lioness.
4   What weapon did Rocky seize when he saw the lioness?
5   How far away from Rocky was the lioness when it started to walk towards him?
6   Why was Rocky unable to see the chest of the lioness?
7   At what part of the animal did Rocky take aim?
8   Where did the bullet hit the ground when Rocky missed the lioness?
9   What did the lioness do after Rocky's shot had missed her?
10 What prevented the lioness from springing upon Rocky?

Sounds

Learn the names of the sounds made by the objects in the list below. Some of the words you learnt in Book 2.

Object	Sound
bugle	call
rain	patter
feet	tramp; shuffle
gun	boom
hoofs	thunder; clatter
paper	rustle; crackle
saw	buzz
steam	hiss
train	rumble
whistle	shriek

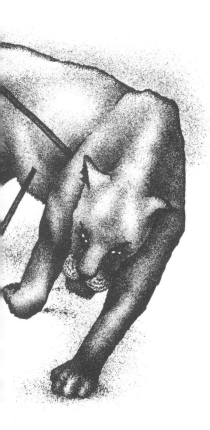

Write the missing words.

A

1 the rumble of a ____
2 the buzz of a ____
3 the patter of ____
4 the hiss of ____
5 the shriek of a ____
6 the rustle of ____
7 the call of a ____
8 the clatter of ____
9 the tramp of ____
10 the boom of a ____

B

1 the ____ of a clock
2 the ____ of dishes
3 the ____ of leaves
4 the ____ of raindrops
5 the ____ of a whip
6 the ____ of the wind
7 the ____ of a drum
8 the ____ of a kettle
9 the ____ of a door
10 the ____ of a horn

C   Write the words needed to complete these sentences.

1 With a ____ of the whistle the express thundered through the little station.

2 The ____ of a bugle summoned the scouts to dinner.

3 The campers heard the ____ of rain on leaves.

4 The picnickers could hear the ____ of a train in the distance.

5 There was a ____ of steam as the old locomotive pulled up.

6 With a ____ of hoofs the hunt went in pursuit of the fox.

7 The ____ of feet filled the air as the regiment marched along.

8 There was a loud ____ as the circular saw cut through the thick wood.

Analogies

The home of a **horse** is called a **stable**.

The home of a **dog** is called a **kennel**.

The **stable** is to the **horse** what the **kennel** is to the **dog** – a home.

We can express it in this way:

Stable is to **horse**
as
kennel is to **dog**

or

Horse is to **stable**
as
dog is to **kennel**

A   Look at the exercise below. In each line find how the words in each pair are related – homes, gender, opposites, parts of the body, occupations, etc. Then write the missing words.

1   **Horse** is to **stable** as **bee** is to _____ .

2   **Man** is to **woman** as **uncle** is to _____ .

3   **Big** is to **small** as **wide** is to _____ .

4   **Foot** is to **toe** as **hand** is to _____ .

5   **Cat** is to **kitten** as **lion** is to _____ .

6   **Cow** is to **beef** as **calf** is to _____ .

7   **Sheep** is to **wool** as **rabbit** is to _____ .

8   **Dog** is to **paw** as **horse** is to _____ .

B   Write the missing words.

1   **Farmer** is to **pigs** as _____ is to **flowers**.

2   **Shoe** is to **foot** as _____ is to **hand**.

3   **Lion** is to **roar** as _____ is to **trumpet**.

4   **Ankle** is to **leg** as _____ is to **arm**.

5   **Car** is to **garage** as _____ is to **hangar**.

6   **Tea** is to **cup** as _____ is to **glass**.

7   **Bakery** is to **bread** as _____ is to **beer**.

8   **Picture** is to **artist** as _____ is to **sculptor**.

The doers of actions

Here is a list of twenty actions and the words used for the people who do these actions.

Action	Doer
act	actor
beg	beggar
carry	carrier
climb	climber
conquer	conqueror
create	creator
cycle	cyclist
decorate	decorator
inhabit	inhabitant
invent	inventor
kidnap	kidnapper
lodge	lodger
manage	manager
reside	resident
sail	sailor
study	student
supply	supplier
tour	tourist
travel	traveller
war	warrior

A What word is used for:

1 one who climbs?
2 one who supplies?
3 one who studies?
4 one who acts?
5 one who lodges?
6 one who travels?
7 one who sails?
8 one who begs?
9 one who tours?
10 one who creates?

B Write the words needed to complete these sentences. Look at the words in bold type at the end of each line.

1 The ____ had covered fifty kilometres before noon. **cycle**

2 Every ____ in the street signed the protest against higher rents. **reside**

3 The house was papered and painted by a London ____ . **decorate**

4 John Logie Baird was the ____ of television. **invent**

5 Boadicea was a British queen and a brave ____ . **war**

6 The ____ of the bank was most helpful. **manage**

7 The ____ stacked the parcels tidily in his van. **carry**

8 Sir Edmund Hillary and Tensing were the first ____ of Mount Everest. **conqueror**

9 Mr. Giles is the oldest ____ in the village. **inhabit**

10 A reward was offered for the capture of the ____ . **kidnap**

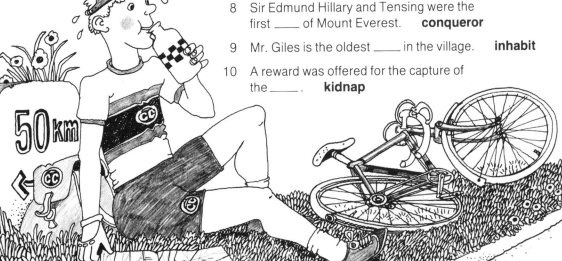

The correct order of sentences

Each of these stories consists of a number of sentences which are not in their correct order. Show, by using numbers, the order in which they should be.

A

1 Mike: "I suppose the wax candle will."

2 Pat: "Wrong, neither of them; they both burn shorter."

3 Pat: "Which will burn longer, a wax candle or a tallow candle?"

B

1 "Of course there is," said his mother, "or why did the little boy burst?"

2 "There's no such thing as too much trifle, Mummy," replied David.

3 "David," said his mother, "did you hear about the little boy who ate too much trifle and burst?"

4 David passed his plate for another helping. "Not enough boy," he chuckled.

5 David started gleefully on his third helping of trifle.

C

1 After a time a wasp landed among the flies and stung him on the nose.

2 "Shoo!" he muttered impatiently. "Since some of you can't behave you must all get off my face."

3 A lazy old tramp lay on the grass in the warm sunshine.

4 At this he raised one dirty hand and rubbed it all over his dirty face.

5 His face was covered with flies, for he was too lazy to drive them off.

D

1 "Well, don't you call that an accident?"

2 A man was being examined by a doctor.

3 "No, sir! He did it on purpose."

4 "Have you ever had an accident?" asked the doctor.

5 "Never, sir," replied the man, "except when a bull tossed me over a fence."

Abbreviations

Here is another list of abbreviations, or short ways of writing words. Learn them thoroughly, then answer the questions.

A.D.	In the year of Our Lord
B.C.	Before Christ
Capt.	Captain
Dept.	Department
do.	ditto – the same
E.R.	Queen Elizabeth
H.M.	Her Majesty
H.M.S.	Her Majesty's Ship
p.	page; pence
P.O.	Post Office Postal Order
P.T.O.	Please turn over
R.A.F.	Royal Air Force

A   Give the meanings of these abbreviations.

1	E.R.	7	P.O.
2	p.	8	Capt.
3	B.C.	9	P.T.O.
4	Dept.	10	do.
5	H.M.	11	R.A.F.
6	A.D.	12	H.M.S.

B   What do the abbreviations in these sentences stand for?

1   Julius Caesar invaded Britain in 55 **B.C.**

2   Uncle Steve is now serving in **H.M.S.** Eagle.

3   **Capt.** Scott commanded the ship *Discovery* which explored the Antarctic.

4   An amusing cartoon appears on **p.** 25.

5   Big alterations are being carried out in the Toy **Dept.**

6   **H.M.** the Queen received a rousing welcome.

7   America was discovered in **A.D.** 1492.

8   Enclosed in the letter was a **P.O.** for 50p.

9   Mr. Gibson is a flying officer in the **R.A.F.**

10   One book at £1.25, **do.** at £1.40.

Tom Sawyer and Aunt Polly

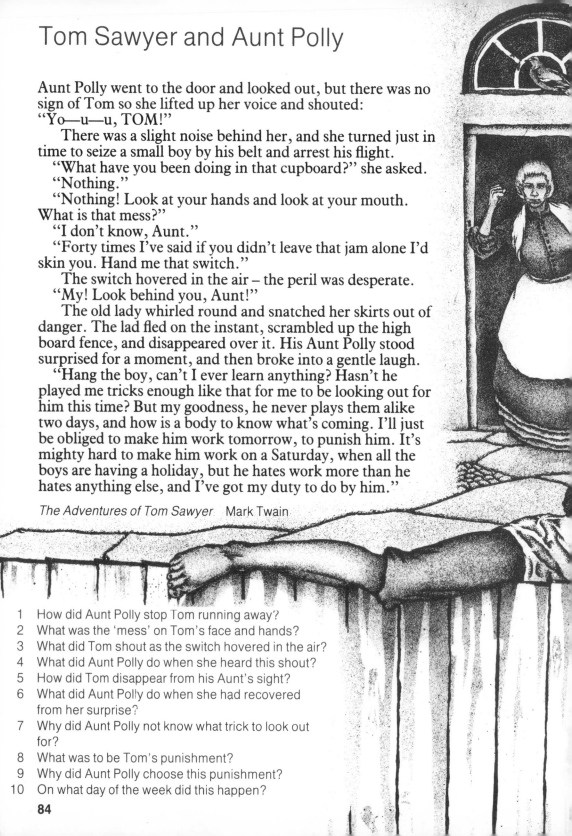

Aunt Polly went to the door and looked out, but there was no sign of Tom so she lifted up her voice and shouted:
"Yo—u—u, TOM!"

There was a slight noise behind her, and she turned just in time to seize a small boy by his belt and arrest his flight.

"What have you been doing in that cupboard?" she asked.
"Nothing."

"Nothing! Look at your hands and look at your mouth. What is that mess?"

"I don't know, Aunt."

"Forty times I've said if you didn't leave that jam alone I'd skin you. Hand me that switch."

The switch hovered in the air – the peril was desperate.
"My! Look behind you, Aunt!"

The old lady whirled round and snatched her skirts out of danger. The lad fled on the instant, scrambled up the high board fence, and disappeared over it. His Aunt Polly stood surprised for a moment, and then broke into a gentle laugh.

"Hang the boy, can't I ever learn anything? Hasn't he played me tricks enough like that for me to be looking out for him this time? But my goodness, he never plays them alike two days, and how is a body to know what's coming. I'll just be obliged to make him work tomorrow, to punish him. It's mighty hard to make him work on a Saturday, when all the boys are having a holiday, but he hates work more than he hates anything else, and I've got my duty to do by him."

The Adventures of Tom Sawyer Mark Twain

1 How did Aunt Polly stop Tom running away?
2 What was the 'mess' on Tom's face and hands?
3 What did Tom shout as the switch hovered in the air?
4 What did Aunt Polly do when she heard this shout?
5 How did Tom disappear from his Aunt's sight?
6 What did Aunt Polly do when she had recovered from her surprise?
7 Why did Aunt Polly not know what trick to look out for?
8 What was to be Tom's punishment?
9 Why did Aunt Polly choose this punishment?
10 On what day of the week did this happen?

Rhymes

eat
bush
lurch
hedge
neat
force
thrush
perch
sedge
course

A Write the words from the list on the left which fill the spaces in the following lines of poetry.

Winter

Sweet blackbird is silenced with chaffinch and ____ , 1
Only waistcoated robin still chirps in the ____ : 2
Soft sun-loving swallows have mustered in ____ , 3
And winged to the spice-teeming southlands
their ____ . 4
Plump housekeeper dormouse had tucked
himself ____ , 5
Just a brown ball in moss with a morsel to ____ : 6
Armed hedgehog has huddled him into the ____ , 7
While frogs scarce miss freezing deep down in
the ____ . 8
Soft swallows have left us alone in the ____ , 9
But robin sits whistling to us from his ____ . 10

B Each of the words missing from these sentences rhymes with the word in bold type.

1 The full-back was penalized for ____ play. **howl**

2 He ____ every word he said. **tent**

3 After the match crowds swarmed on to
the ____ . **healed**

4 I ____ if I shall be able to come. **shout**

5 The man was charged at the local
police ____ . **port**

6 This room requires a new ____ of furniture. **beat**

C The three words in each group rhyme with the word in bold type. Write the rhyming words.

1 **late**

w____
aw____
cr____

2 **share**

desp____
decl____
sw____

3 **bean**

cant____
mach____
sc____

4 **rain**

cr____
ch____
sk____

5 **bite**

fr____
h____
sp____

85

More fun with words

A   Rearrange the letters of each word in bold type to complete the sentences.

Example
The **bleat** was made of solid oak.
The **table** was made of solid oak.

1   The famous actress first appeared on the **gates** when she was only six.

2   Captain Smith has a long, black **bread**.

3   Whilst picking blackberries Paul got a **north** in his finger.

4   Jim helped to pick the ripe **lumps**.

5   Uncle Tom was a **valse** on a cotton plantation.

6   A huge **could** darkened the sky.

7   The **plates** of the buttercup are yellow.

8   A large crowd watched the soldiers **charm** through the town.

9   The customer refused to take the **least** loaf of bread.

B   In each group below the second word of each pair is formed by inserting a letter after the first letter of the first word.

Example

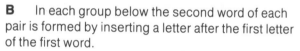

cat	coat		cat	c**o**at
lad	load		lad	l**o**ad
hard	____		hard	h**o**ard

The letter **o** has been inserted.

Find the letter to be inserted in each group, then write the missing words in your exercise book.

1	sock	smock	2	fag	flag	3	bad	bead
	sell	smell		beak	bleak		fast	feast
	sash	____		pain	____		cram	____

4	pay	pray	5	sand	stand	6	lid	laid
	band	brand		sick	stick		pin	pain
	fight	____		sole	____		pint	____

7	sake	shake	8	sat	spat	9	sum	scum
	coke	choke		send	spend		sold	scold
	soot	____		soil	____		sent	____

Proverbs

Learn these proverbs and their meanings before attempting the questions which follow.

Birds of a feather flock together	People of similar tastes enjoy one another's company.
Cut your coat according to your cloth	Learn to live within your means.
Fine feathers make fine birds	Fine clothes make a person look important, although he may not be.
Two heads are better than one	Two people together may solve a problem which one alone cannot.
Waste not, want not	Be thrifty and you may never be in need.
One good turn deserves another	People who are kind to others deserve the same treatment themselves.

A Write these proverbs, filling in the missing words.

1 ____ not, ____ not.

2 Two ____ are better than ____ .

3 Fine ____ make fine ____ .

4 One good ____ deserves ____ .

5 Cut your ____ according to your ____ .

B Write the proverbs which these sentences suggest.

1 She dresses and looks like a duchess although she is only a servant.

2 If you earn £50 a week you should not spend more than £50 a week.

3 Perhaps you can help me to solve this problem.

4 Smith, Brown and Johnson are great friends; all are keen on music.

5 Carol mended Ian's socks so Ian cooked the lunch.

Similes

When something is very **light** in weight we say it is **as light as a feather**.

This is because it is similar to a feather in **weight**.

Learn the sayings in this list, then answer the questions.

as light as a feather
as cunning as a fox
as flat as a pancake
as fresh as a daisy
as old as the hills
as poor as a church mouse
as proud as a peacock
as quick as lightning
as safe as houses
as steady as a rock

A Write the missing words.

1 as steady as a ____
2 as proud as a ____
3 as poor as a ____
4 as flat as a ____
5 as quick as ____

6 as safe as ____
7 as light as a ____
8 as fresh as a ____
9 as old as the ____
10 as cunning as a ____

B

1 as ____ as lightning
2 as ____ as a pancake
3 as ____ as houses
4 as ____ as a daisy
5 as ____ as the hills
6 as ____ as a rock
7 as ____ as a church mouse
8 as ____ as a fox
9 as ____ as a peacock
10 as ____ as a feather

C Write the saying which fits each picture.

D What are the missing words?

1 Our cricket field is as flat as a ____ .

2 This hat is as old as the ____ .

3 The old oak table was as steady as a ____ .

4 After losing his fortune Dick was as poor as a ____ .

5 His movements were as quick as ____ .

Variety in writing sentences

Notice the order of words in this sentence.

A ruined castle stood on top of the hill.

subject first

You will see that the subject, the thing spoken about, comes first.

Now look at this sentence.

On top of the hill stood a **ruined castle**.

subject last

It is natural to put the subject of a sentence first, but by changing this order it is possible to get variety. This makes the writing of sentences much more interesting.

A Rewrite these sentences, beginning with the words in bold type. Don't forget to use a capital letter for the first word.

1 The two boys went to see a film **last** night.

2 The rooks were cawing loudly **up** in the tall trees.

3 My brother decided to become a policeman **because** he is so tall and strong.

4 The carnival was postponed **owing** to the very heavy rain.

5 The village smithy stands **under** a spreading chestnut tree.

B Now do the same with these sentences.

1 Soon after his father died **Michael** emigrated to Canada.

2 Under the railway bridge **a** tramp was sheltering from the rain.

3 Without stopping to look if the road was clear, **Martin** darted across the road.

4 In the nick of time **the** fireman jumped clear of the falling roof.

5 Because he did not work **Roger** failed his exam.

C Write three sentences of your own in which the subject comes first, then rewrite each sentence so that the subject comes last.

The golden fleece

Immediately the fifty heroes got on board, and, seizing their oars, held them perpendicularly in the air, while Orpheus (who liked such a task far better than rowing) swept his fingers across the harp. At the first ringing note of the music they felt the vessel stir. Orpheus thrummed away briskly, and the galley slid at once into the sea, dipping her prow deeply and rising again as buoyant as a swan. Thus triumphantly did the *Argo* sail out of harbour, amidst the good wishes of everybody except the wicked old Pelias, who stood on a promontory scowling at her, and wishing he could blow out of his lungs the tempest of wrath that was in his heart, and so sink the galley with all on board.

To make the time pass more pleasantly during the voyage the heroes talked about the Golden Fleece. It had originally belonged to a ram, who had taken on his back two children, when in danger of their lives, and fled with them over land and sea. One of the children, whose name was Helle, fell into the sea and was drowned. But the other (a little boy named Phrixus) was brought safely ashore by the faithful ram, who, however, was so exhausted that he immediately lay down and died. In memory of this good deed the fleece of the poor dead ram was miraculously changed to gold. It was hung upon a tree in a sacred grove, where it had now been kept for many years, and was the envy of mighty kings, who had nothing so magnificent in any of their palaces.

Tanglewood Tales   Nathaniel Hawthorne

1   How many heroes went aboard the *Argo*?
2   What did Orpheus like doing far better than rowing?
3   What did the heroes feel at the first ringing note of the music?
4   Where was Pelias standing when the *Argo* left harbour?
5   What did he wish he could do to the ship?
6   How did the heroes make the time pass more pleasantly during the voyage?
7   How did Helle die?
8   What happened to Phrixus?
9   What change came over the fleece of the ram after its death?
10   Where was the ram's fleece kept?

ANSWERS

Page 1 Nouns

A
1 box; wood
2 apples; dish
3 milk; weather
4 lion; shade; tree
5 butter; milk
6 usherette; ticket
7 oranges; marmalade
8 dog; food
9 winter; days; nights
10 children; visit; zoo

B
1 altar
2 burrow
3 century
4 drake
5 eaves
6 fable
7 giraffe
8 hammer
9 island
10 junction

Page 2 Verbs

A
1 washed; hung
2 tries; makes
3 folded; placed
4 finished; cleaned
5 takes; walk
6 wrote; posted
7 looked; disappeared
8 flopped; grunted

B
1 welcomed
2 sniffed
3 galloped
4 wriggled
5 repaired
6 trickled
7 shuffled
8 trampled

Page 3 Adjectives

A
1 cold; wet
2 little; bright; warm
3 ancient; deep
4 hard; successful
5 slim; graceful; blue; golden
6 Huge; giant
7 warm; comfortable
8 delicious; thick; chocolate

B
1 nourishing
2 stormy
3 happy
4 valuable
5 fatal
6 fashionable
7 savage
8 thrilling
9 tedious
10 loyal

C
Own answers

Page 4   Nouns — formation

A
1 invention
2 information
3 laughter
4 performance
5 loss
6 service
7 division
8 beginning
9 pleasure
10 settlement

B
1 movement
2 intention
3 departure
4 permission
5 composition
6 admiration
7 existence
8 rebellion
9 description
10 persuasion

Page 5   Nouns — number

A

Add -s
chiefs
chimneys
pianos
roofs

Add -es
cargoes
echoes
heroes
potatoes
tomatoes

Change y to i, add -es
batteries
hobbies
replies
supplies

Change f to v, add -es
halves
leaves
loaves
shelves
wolves

Change the vowels
feet
geese
mice
teeth
women

B
1 halves	2 hobbies	3 potatoes
4 sheep	5 bullies	6 tomatoes
7 leaves	8 chimneys	9 pianos
10 wolves	11 replies	12 geese

C
1 foot	2 hero	3 loaf
4 supply	5 mouse	6 shelf
7 echo	8 woman	9 toe
10 tooth	11 battery	12 swine

Page 6 Sinbad and the coconuts

1 The merchant gave Sinbad a large bag in which to carry the coconuts.
2 Sinbad wondered how they would get the coconuts off the trees because the trees were so tall.
3 The men threw stones at the monkeys in the trees.
4 The monkeys threw coconuts at the men in return.
5 The men filled their bags with the coconuts.
6 The throwing continued for several days.
7 Sinbad's voyage ended in Baghdad.
8 Sinbad had done well by changing his coconuts for pearls and spices in the places at which he called on the voyage.

Page 7 Verbs — past tense and participle

A
1 swam
2 beat
3 shook
4 wrote
5 bled
6 held

B
1 thrown
2 forgotten
3 beaten
4 written
5 swum
6 shaken

Page 8 Comparing adjectives

1 coarsest
4 wisest
7 wider
10 shadier

2 coldest
5 purest
8 sunniest

3 slimmer
6 thinnest
9 bigger

Page 9 Words to complete words

A
1 batch
2 waste
3 carols
4 capture
5 cupboard
6 figures
7 cattle
8 penalty
9 antler
10 vanish

B
1 burden
2 magnet
3 combat
4 lesson
5 croak
6 tyrant
7 blink
8 target
9 manage
10 carpet

Page 10 Using words correctly

A

1 passed
2 past
3 passed
4 passed
5 past
6 past
7 passed
8 past

B

1 its
2 it's
3 it's
4 its
5 its
6 it's
7 its; it's
8 it's; its

Page 11 Alphabetical order

A

bag
coat
hatstand
lamp
mirror
piano
table
umbrella

B

1 active
broad
doubt
lenient
youth

2 chemist
eastern
grab
justice
kneel

3 haughty
month
nothing
skilful
unicorn

C

1 panic
perch
plank
press
punch

2 canter
centre
cheat
clever
crisp

3 gander
geese
goose
grape
guilty

D

1 deadly
debtor
decide
defeat
demand

2 habit
hamper
harmful
hatch
haunt

3 prank
prepare
price
produce
prune

Page 12   The crows and the snake

1 The snake used to eat the young birds as soon as they were hatched.
2 The snake was much stronger than the crows.
3 The king's son came down to the river the following day.
4 He came to the river to swim.
5 The crow took the lovely gold anklet which the prince had taken off.
6 He hid it in the hollow tree in which the crows had their nest.
7 The servants found the cruel snake and killed it.
8 The crows were able to bring up their family in peace after this because there was no snake to eat their young ones.

Page 13   Gender

	A		B		C		D
1	heroine	1	actor	1	duchess	1	earl
2	bitch	2	bridegroom	2	goose	2	cockerel
3	vixen	3	gander	3	mare	3	bridegroom
4	nun	4	cockerel	4	landlady	4	dogs
5	princess	5	emperor				
6	countess	6	landlord				
7	actress	7	stallion				
8	daughter	8	headmaster				
9	headmistress	9	tiger				
10	hostess	10	duke				
11	mare	11	fox				
12	empress	12	monk				

Page 14   Letter writing

Own answers.

Page 15   Adjectives — formation

	A		B		C
1	thirsty	1	icy	1	muddy
2	sleepy	2	rosy	2	sunny
3	inky	3	juicy	3	fatty
4	cloudy	4	shady	4	starry
5	crusty	5	smoky	5	baggy
6	stormy	6	greasy	6	funny

Page 16   Same sound – different meaning

A

flour
whole
hole
grate
piece

B

1   been; beans
2   peace; piece
3   him; hymn
4   bawl; ball

Page 17   People

A

volunteer
widower
bankrupt
orphan
hostess

B

1   bachelor
2   ancestor
3   blackleg
4   bully
5   guests

Page 18   The Princess and the pea

The Prince wanted to marry a real Princess.
During the terrible storm there was a knocking at the gate of the town.
The old King went to open the gate.
A Princess stood outside the gate.
The Queen put a small pea on the slabs of the bed.
On top of this she put twenty mattresses and twenty eiderdown beds.
The Princess slept very badly that night.
Her body was black and blue next morning.

Page 19   Collective nouns

A

set
sheaf
party
herd
bunch
gang
library
swarm

9   whales
10   oxen
11   fish
12   furniture
13   elephants
14   monkeys
15   kittens
16   islands

B

1   school
2   gang
3   herd
4   shoal
5   suite
6   team
7   group
8   swarm
9   litter

Page 20 Forming adjectives from nouns

A

1	woollen	11	angry
2	hasty	12	marvellous
3	favourite	13	customary
4	natural	14	musical
5	poisonous	15	dangerous
6	affectionate	16	expensive
7	furious	17	courageous
8	heroic	18	friendly
9	victorious	19	famous
10	central	20	valuable

B

1 heroic
2 favourite
3 marvellous
4 valuable
5 expensive
6 customary
7 poisonous
8 natural
9 affectionate
10 friendly

Page 21 Pronouns

A

1 he; him
2 it
3 they
4 She; them
5 she; her

B

1 him
2 she
3 us; we
4 you
5 he; her; her
6 his

Page 22 Fun with words

A

1	twine	6	place
2	sold	7	crash
3	reach	8	flock
4	wedge	9	shark
5	brain		

B

1	thin	6	lead
2	diet	7	charm
3	race	8	leapt
4	cast	9	least
5	bush	10	spoilt

Page 23 Using capital letters

A

1 Ian saw the Houses of Parliament and Buckingham Palace.
2 I shall be on holiday on Saturday the 29th of July.
3 We are moving to 24 Richmond Road, Swansea.
4 If all the seas were one sea,
   What a great sea there would be!
5 Easter Monday is the Monday after Good Friday.
6 Jean has read Oliver Twist and Black Beauty.

B
Own answers.

Page 24 Aladdin

Mustafa lived in one of the large cities of China.
Mustafa was a tailor.
Mustafa had one child.
Aladdin was naughty, lazy and disobedient.
Aladdin played in the streets from morning till night.
Mustafa took Aladdin into his own shop and showed him how to use a needle.
Aladdin could not settle down to work because he had had his own way for so long.
His father got so angry that he became ill and soon died.
Aladdin's mother sold all the things that were in the shop.
Aladdin's mother earned money by spinning cotton.

Page 25 Direct speech

A
"Pass me the butter, Carol," said her mother.
"Would you like another cake?" asked Mrs. Brown.
"These eggs are not fresh," complained the customer.
"Is this the way to Norfolk, please?" inquired the walker.
"Look out below," shouted the steeplejack.
"Please do all you can to help us," cried Old Tom.
"The meeting is now closed," declared the chairman.
"Pick your feet up," the sergeant-major shouted to the recruits.
"I am the best bowler in the team," boasted Andrew.
"Don't let me catch you throwing stones again, Peter," warned his father.

B
Own answers.

Page 26 Occupations

A		B		C
optician	1	typist	1	fruiterer
judge	2	judge	2	confectioner
chemist	3	footballer	3	fishmonger
footballer	4	artist	4	chemist
pianist	5	optician	5	butcher
chef	6	air hostess	6	grocer
fruiterer				
carpenter				

Page 27   Proper adjectives

A
1 Scottish
2 British
3 Irish
4 English
5 French
6 Egyptian
7 Russian

B
1 Italian
2 German
3 Japanese
4 Russian
5 Canadian
6 Egyptian
7 French

C
Own answers.

Page 28   Using words correctly — revision

A
1 saw
2 seen
3 is
4 are
5 two; too; to

B
1 ate
2 eaten
3 taken
4 took
5 hear
6 There; their
7 gave
8 given
9 did
10 done

Page 29   Group names

A
1 seasons
4 counties
7 occupations
10 months
2 weapons
5 entertainments
8 rivers
11 games (pastimes)
3 letters
6 numbers
9 headgear
12 buildings

B
1 insect
2 bird
3 animal

C

Fish	Flowers	Groceries	Trees
salmon	daffodil	tea	beech
hake	snowdrop	butter	elm
mackerel	bluebell	lard	oak
herring	daisy	cheese	ash
plaice	tulip	sugar	birch
cod	pansy	margarine	sycamore

Page 30   A find for Carlos

1 The puppy had not learned to use her tongue.
2 Carlos passed some cottages on his way to the puppy.
3 Carlos had wandered out because he was bored and curious.
4 He was too new to the district to have made any friends.
5 Carlos's brother thought him too young to share his interests and pastimes.

Carlos thought he might find frogs or lizards in the crack in the ground.
He expected to find these because there was a little bit of grass and a few flowers.
Carlos knew that the puppy was alive because he saw her flanks heave.
He was sure that the puppy had no owner because of her bedraggled condition and the deserted place where she was found.
Carlos wanted to leave the place as soon as possible in case someone came for the puppy.

Page 31 Joining sentences

A
Katy washed the car and polished it until it shone.
John took off his shoes and socks and paddled in the sea.
The goalkeeper jumped high and punched the ball away.

B
The dog chased the cat but failed to catch her.
She slipped and fell but did not hurt herself.
Fire destroyed the factory but no lives were lost.

C
The tap was frozen so we could get no water.
He could not spell the word so he looked it up in his dictionary.
Jane had measles so she could not go to the party.
Stephen spent his bus fare on sweets so he had to walk home.

D
He could not walk because he had sprained his ankle.
David had a bad headache so he went to bed early.
Louise went to the dentist and had two teeth filled.
I enjoy going swimming but I do not like cold water.

Page 32 Opposites using un, in, im

A
				B	
insecure	11	insufficient		1	untruthful
unselfish	12	unhealthy		2	insufficient
impure	13	immovable		3	invisible
uncommon	14	unused		4	unhealthy
incapable	15	invisible		5	unselfish
uncertain	16	unsteady		6	incomplete
indirect	17	impossible		7	immovable
unpleasant	18	unsuitable		8	incurable
inconvenient	19	unwise		9	incorrect
incorrect	20	incomplete		10	unconscious

Page 33　People

A
1　truant
2　daredevil
3　coward
4　pilgrim
5　spendthrift

B
1　miser
2　glutton
3　hermit
4　cannibals
5　patriot

Page 34　Opposites using dis

A
1　disagree
2　disallow
3　disbelieve
4　disadvantage
5　discomfort
6　discontented
7　disfavour
8　dishonest
9　dislike
10　disloyal
11　disorder
12　displeased
13　disrespect
14　dissatisfied
15　distaste
16　distrust

B
1　discontented
2　dislike
3　discomfort
4　dissatisfied
5　disrespect

C
1　dishonest
2　disadvantage
3　distrust
4　disorder
5　disagree

Page 35　Nouns — possession

A
1　a kangaroo's tail
2　the sheep's wool
3　a donkey's ears
4　an eagle's beak
5　a pig's snout
6　the lion's tail

B
1　a boys' school
2　a robins' nest
3　a girls' playground
4　a dogs' home
5　a soldiers' camp
6　the elephants' trunks
7　the cows' tails
8　a teachers' meeting
9　the pirates' treasure
10　the rabbits' burrows

C
Own answers.

Page 36　Pinocchio and the policeman

1　Geppetto placed the marionette on the floor to see if he could walk.
2　Pinocchio was unable to walk because his legs were stiff.
3　Geppetto took Pinocchio by the hand and showed him how to put one foot before the other.
4　After learning to walk and run Pinocchio slipped out of the door into the street and ran away.
5　Geppetto could not catch him because Pinocchio jumped like a rabbit.

6 When the people saw Pinocchio running they stared in amazement and then laughed until their sides were sore.
7 The policeman thought that somebody's horse had got away from its master.
8 When Pinocchio tried to run between the policeman's legs he failed, and the policeman picked him up by his nose and returned him to Geppetto.
9 Geppetto intended to punish Pinocchio by pulling his ears.
0 He was unable to carry out this punishment because in his hurry he had forgotten to make Pinocchio's ears.

Page 37 Contractions

A

1 we've
2 I'm
3 they're
4 you've
5 I've
6 we're
7 you're
8 they've

B

1 they're
2 it's
3 I've
4 you'll
5 I'm
6 we'll
7 you've
8 he's
9 we're
10 I'll

11 we've
12 they'll
13 you're
14 she'll
15 they've
16 isn't
17 she's
18 can't
19 he'll
20 haven't

Page 38 Opposites

A

1 less
2 tough
3 noisy
4 blunt
5 idle
6 worse
7 foolish
8 light
9 narrow
0 above

11 shallow
12 good
13 bright
14 cruel
15 dead
16 asleep
17 sober
18 sorry
19 dear
20 smooth

B

1 cheap
2 busy
3 deep
4 below
5 dull
6 tender
7 wise
8 alive
9 drunk
10 rough

Page 39 Direct speech

A

1 Sally's mother warned her, "Keep away from the fire!"
2 The boatman shouted, "Any more for the Skylark, please?"
3 People in the audience were yelling, "More! We want more!"
4 Before leaving, Anita said, "Thank you for a lovely holiday, Aunt Muriel."

5   Mr. Paul asked, "Will you play in goal, Raymond?"

B
1   Peter shouted, "I can't hear what you say."
2   The teacher said, "Put your books away, everybody."
3   The milkman muttered, "My feet are icy cold."
4   Mrs. Polly asked, "Would anyone like another cup of tea?"
5   Richard inquired, "Is this the way to the hospital?"

C
1   "Three tries for 20p," shouted the showman.
2   "There's a big storm blowing up," remarked the old sailor.
3   "I'm afraid my leg is broken," muttered the full-back with a groan.
4   "Thank goodness there are no more exams!" exclaimed Robin.
5   "Hush, David's sleeping," Jennifer's mother whispered.

Page 40   Compound words

A
1   foot + path = footpath
2   rain + bow = rainbow
3   scare + crow = scarecrow
4   sign + post = signpost
5   water + fall = waterfall
6   wind + mill = windmill

B
1   sunlight
2   wallpaper
3   headmaster
4   mudguard
5   flagpole
6   broomstick
7   farmyard
8   nightdress
9   classroom
10   playground

Page 41   Young ones

A
1   puppy; pup
2   lamb
3   cub
4   kitten
5   kid
6   duckling
7   calf
8   chick
9   eaglet
10   fawn

B
1   cubs
2   puppies
3   kittens
4   chicks
5   lamb
6   kids
7   ducklings
8   eaglets
9   calf
10   fawn

Page 42   Heidi in the mountains

Heidi was awakened early next morning by a loud whistle.
The sun seemed to turn everything in the attic to gold.
Peter was waiting outside the hut.
Peter had a flock of goats with him.
Peter stopped at the hut to take Alm-Uncle's goats with his.
Heidi's grandfather told her to wash and make herself tidy before going off with the goats.
He had put a large tub of water for Heidi to wash herself.
The names of the grandfather's goats were Little Swan and Little Bear.
The old man put a large piece of bread and a lump of cheese in the wallet.
Heidi would have goats' milk with her dinner.

Page 43   Adverbs

A	B	
plainly	1 roughly	9 madly
soundly	2 vainly	10 ably
politely	3 cosily	11 haughtily
patiently	4 terribly	12 loudly
rudely	5 jokingly	13 hastily
heartily	6 equally	14 pitifully
distinctly	7 noisily	15 sensibly
bitterly	8 singly	16 nimbly

Plus own answers.

Page 44   Joining sentences

A
Mr. Dale has two daughters who are very much alike.
James found the book which Richard had lost.
The police were looking for a man who had set fire to a factory.
Jane was given a ring which had belonged to her grandmother.
David and I met a soldier who had been awarded the V.C.
At the museum we saw a uniform which had been worn by Lord Nelson.
Mr. and Mrs. Harris adopted the two children who had no one to care for them.
Androcles approached the lion which had a thorn in its paw.

B
She tried the hat on but it was too small.
The wounded soldier was cheerful although he was in pain.
I shall be cross unless you tell me the truth.
He was absent from school because he had a bad cold.
The collector took Janet's ticket and punched it.
I will come to see you before you go abroad.

7 You may come with me if you promise to be good.
8 The girls watched television while their mother went to the dentist.
9 It was so cold that the ponds were frozen.
10 Put some coal on the fire or it will soon be out.

Page 45   Describing things

A
Own answers.

B
Own answers.

C
Own answers.

Page 46   Proverbs

A
1 Make hay while the sun shines.
2 Too many cooks spoil the broth.
3 Look before you leap.
4 The early bird catches the worm.

B
1 Look before you leap.
2 Don't count your chickens before they are hatched.
3 Empty vessels make most noise.
4 Too many cooks spoil the broth.

Page 47   Same sound – different meaning

A
1 beat
2 yolk
3 peal
4 bough
5 cell

B
1 haul; hall
2 need; knead
3 time; thyme
4 ring; wring
5 feet; feat

Page 48   Doctor Goldsmith's medicine

1 Goldsmith was sometimes called Doctor because he had studied medicine.
2 He had little money left himself because he gave away so much to the poor.
3 The poor woman asked Goldsmith to come to see her husband who was sick and would not eat any food.
4 The woman's family was poor because the man had had no work for a considerable time.
5 Goldsmith told the woman to come and see him that evening.
6 Goldsmith gave the woman a small box which was quite heavy for its size.
7 Goldsmith asked the woman not to open the box until she got home.
8 Goldsmith told the woman she would find full directions for taking the medicine inside the box.
9 The medicine the box contained was money.
10 The directions given with the medicine were: "To be taken as often as necessity requires."

Page 49   Direct and indirect speech

A

1 Mr. Findlay remarked that the days were getting longer.
2 Mrs. Gray asked John if he had trimmed the hedges.
3 Nigel explained that he was late because of the rain.
4 Fred urged Michael to have another sweet.
5 Alison's mother told her to poke the fire.
6 Colin's father warned him not to go skating on the pond.

B

1 "I am really tired, mother," said Philip.
2 "It is a glorious day," remarked the landlady.
3 "I am going to have my dinner, Stephen," said Ian.
4 "I expect better work from you in future, David," said his teacher.
5 "I shall be leaving at the end of the term," announced the headmaster.
6 "Would you like to come to the cinema with me, Anne?" asked Derek.

Page 50   Abbreviations

A

1 British Rail
2 General Post Office
3 afternoon
4 horse power; hire-purchase
5 British Broadcasting Corporation
6 and other things
7 kilometres per hour
8 before noon
9 Do It Yourself
10 Company
11 Police Constable
12 Number

B

1 Company
2 hire-purchase
3 and other things
4 British Broadcasting Corporation
5 kilometres per hour
6 Number
7 before noon
8 Police Constable
9 afternoon
10 Do It Yourself

Page 51   Using words correctly

	A		B		C		D
1	whose	1	began	1	broke	1	come
2	who's	2	begun	2	broken	2	come
3	whose	3	begun	3	broken	3	came
4	who's	4	begun	4	broke	4	come
5	whose	5	began	5	broken	5	came
				6	broke		

Page 52 Alphabetical order

A

1. handsome
   print
   tiger
   wheel

2. bathe
   damage
   linger
   manage

3. flour
   gloom
   quiz
   record

B

4. vanish
   vestry
   violet
   vowel
   vulgar

5. abroad
   active
   addition
   affect
   ancient

6. laugh
   leave
   light
   loyal
   luggage

C

7. blank
   bleak
   blink
   block
   blunder

8. change
   cheat
   chilly
   chorus
   church

9. spend
   spice
   splash
   sponge
   spring

D

1. head
   health
   heath
   heave

2. clean
   clench
   clergy
   clever

3. drudge
   drug
   drum
   drunk

4. parcel
   parent
   park
   part

5. bracket
   bramble
   branch
   brawn

6. street
   stripe
   strong
   struck

7. recall
   recent
   recipe
   recruit

8. wheel
   when
   where
   whether

9. excess
   exchange
   excite
   exclaim

Page 53 Similars

A

1. rich
2. help
3. empty
4. lucky
5. hide
6. top
7. huge
8. middle
9. plentiful
10. enough

B

1	waste	2	careful
4	leave	5	disappear
7	pitiful	8	rash

3 stubborn
6 famous
9 slim

Page 54   Michael at the clinic

1 A red-haired nurse took Michael's name.
2 She remarked that Doctor would probably discharge him that day.
3 Michael's scowl returned.
4 When the nurse left him Michael was scuffing his shoes against the bar of a chair in the waiting room.
5 The doctor made Michael turn his wrist from side to side.
6 When the doctor gripped Michael's arm he told him to waggle his fingers and thumb.
7 Michael's arm had had a cracked bone.
8 Last week's X-ray showed that the cracked bone had healed perfectly.
9 Michael had to go back to school on the Monday after the Whit week half-term.
10 The doctor told Michael to be careful of his arm at first.

Page 55   Occupations

A
1 newsagent
2 decorator
3 cashier
4 bricklayer
5 bookseller
6 cameraman
7 salesman
8 veterinary surgeon

B
1 bricklayer
2 reporter
3 bank clerk
4 potter
5 bookseller
6 cashier
7 decorator
8 salesman
9 model
10 umpire

C
1 shepherd
2 jockey
3 newsagent

Page 56   Prepositions

1	off	2	into
4	under	5	across
7	in	8	before
10	behind		

3 over
6 on
9 near

Page 57   Forming nouns from verbs

A
1 allowance
2 defence
3 delivery
4 injury
5 action
6 entrance
7 marriage
8 production
9 pressure
10 success

B
1 behaviour
2 remainder
3 discovery
4 growth
5 invitation
6 obedience
7 arrival
8 defiance
9 knowledge

Page 58   Verbs — past tense and participle

1 wound
2 sawn
3 sewed
4 mowed
5 trodden
6 sewn
7 knelt
8 sprung
9 sprang
10 sworn
11 swollen
12 bought

Page 59   Fun with words

A
1 wage
2 firm
3 bunk
4 heart
5 cloth
6 grind
7 earl
8 boar
9 song

B
1 grind
2 sole
3 fine
4 come
5 thing
6 slink
7 spade
8 bird
9 larder

Page 60   Sir Henry springs a visit

1 This story is set in the year 1815.
2 The incident takes place in Italy.
3 Ben chose the Spanish Steps because they were near the hotel and because there was so much life and movement there.
4 Ben could see the western skyline with the Vatican and the long Janiculum ridge stretched out in front.
5 The Steps was an ideal place for an artist to work because there were always many people to draw and he could sell his work there.
6 A lightning sketch means a very quick sketch; one done in a very short time.
7 Ben had previously lived in London.
8 Ben was also a servant of Sir Henry's.
9 The tourist had been about to buy the sketch of a Flower Girl.
10 Sir Henry was so angry because he thought his friends would be asking if he did not pay Ben enough.

Page 61 The doers of actions

A

1 bowler
2 singer
3 weaver
4 builder
5 drummer
6 boxer
7 grumbler
8 winner
9 explorer
10 settler

B

1 boxer
2 straggler
3 diver
4 shopper
5 gardener
6 toddler
7 runner
8 gambler
9 performer
10 striker

Page 62 Adjectives

A

mountainous country
scorching heat
deafening shout
shabby clothes
fragrant flower
gigantic strength
intelligent pupil
hoarse voice
ferocious tiger
devoted mother

B

1 wholesome
2 frequent
3 deadly
4 rugged
5 strenuous
6 celebrated
7 fragile
8 tarnished
9 forbidding
10 boundless

C

Own answers.

Page 63 Punctuation

1 Have you ever spent a holiday abroad?
2 Yes, I went to Spain last summer.
3 Hold tight! The brakes are not working!
4 Now, where was I before I was interrupted?
5 Please lock up before you go, Philip.
6 Oh! Look at that dear little rabbit!
7 Jennifer, have you finished your homework?
8 Cyprus, Corsica, Malta, Elba and Sicily are all islands.

Page 64 Rhymes

A

1 world
2 curled
3 breast
4 dressed
5 me
6 tree
7 mills
8 hills
9 go
10 flow
11 isles
12 miles

B

1 freeze
2 scene
3 worse
4 crumb
5 cloak
6 plough

C

In the dark and lonely night,
When the stars are all alight,
Sleep comes creeping up the street,
With her naked, silent feet,
Carrying upon her back
Dreams of all kinds in a sack

Page 65   Words with more than one meaning

A

1 check	2 stamp	3 train	4 sound
5 stone	6 hiding	7 swallow	8 score
9 lock	10 spoke		

B
Own answers.

Page 66   Lucy comes to Hagworthy

1 Three people got off the train.
2 Lucy had a 'sudden sinking feeling' because she could see no one there to meet her and wondered if her father had made a muddle over the day.
3 The car park was reached from the station by a flight of steps.
4 It was five years since Lucy had seen Aunt Mabel.
5 Aunt Mabel was short-sighted.
6 The words 'heaving a little as she got her breath back' tell us that Aunt Mabel was probably plump.
7 They felt awkward when they kissed because they had not seen each other for such a long time.
8 Aunt Mabel's full name was Miss Mabel Clough.
9 She had accepted her niece completely, without question as if she were another piece of luggage like the crate or the parcel.
0 Aunt Mabel was forgetful, untidy and disorganised.

Page 67   Opposites

A

1 found	2 rough	3 enemy; foe
4 shallow	5 many	6 above
7 first	8 tender	9 loose
0 idle	11 seldom	12 alive
3 forget	14 dear	15 narrow
6 foolish	17 sink	18 sober
9 coward	20 dull	

B
1 sink
4 loose
7 wide
10 few

2 hero
5 last
8 forgot

3 enemies; foes
6 found
9 often

Page 68 Subject and predicate

A
1 A bank of cloud   covered the sun.
2 Our new teacher   has wavy brown hair.
3 The whole family   goes to church on Sundays.
4 The two chimpanzees   escaped from the zoo.
5 The rough seas   capsized the little boat.

B
1 The stationmaster explained why the train was late.
2 Meat and vegetables make a satisfying meal.
3 The plane took off despite the bad weather.
4 The clever dog walked on his hind legs.
5 The lonely cottage is said to be haunted.

C
Own answers.

D
Own answers.

Page 69 Agreement of subject and verb

1 makes
4 does
7 take

2 cleans
5 put
8 is

3 has
6 make
9 do

Page 70 Words to complete words

A
1 cardigan
2 century
3 chapter
4 partner
5 balloon
6 factory
7 massage
8 earnest

B
1 remark
2 bridle
3 bargain
4 reward
5 consent
6 translate
7 support
8 oblong
9 escape

Page 71   Same sound – different meaning

A

1	four; fore	2	steel	3	reign
4	dye	5	seam	6	waste; waist
7	pray	8	write; right	9	stair; stare

B

1	cell	2	bawl	3	knead
4	leek	5	beet	6	peal
7	grate	8	feat	9	fir
10	bough	11	wring	12	haul
13	whole	14	thyme	15	bean
16	flour	17	hymn	18	yoke
19	piece	20	mail		

Page 72   International airport

1 A modern international airport may be compared in size with a small town.
2 The function of an airport is to process through its system hundreds of thousands of aircraft movements, millions of passengers and many tons of freight.
3 The task of the air-traffic controller is to take charge of all taking-off and landing movements.
4 The controller operates from a control tower.
5 Airborne planes are contacted by radar.
6 Radar assists the controller by enabling him to see the aircraft's position in the air.
7 The task of customs officials is to check that certain goods do not go out of or come into the country without their knowledge.
8 Meals for passengers are pre-packed because facilities for preparing for such large numbers would take up too much space on the aircraft.
9 Maintenance engineers are responsible for the safety of the aircraft.
10 Aeroplanes are specially fitted out to carry freight by removing the seats and replacing them with special freight fasteners.

Page 73   Common sayings

1 to let the **cat** out of the **bag**;   to give away a secret.
2 to get into **hot** water;   to get into trouble.
3 to make both **ends** meet;   to live within one's means.
4 to paddle one's own **canoe**;   to do things for oneself.
5 to have a **feather** in one's cap;   to have done something to be proud of.
6 to hit below the **belt**;   to act unfairly towards an opponent.
7 to **hang** one's head;   to be ashamed of oneself.
8 to have a **bone** to **pick** with someone;   to have a dispute to settle or a complaint to make.
9 to turn over a new **leaf**;   to lead a new life.
10 to put the **cart** before the **horse**;   to do things the wrong way round.

Page 74 Similars

A
			B
inquire	ask	1	kind
necessity	need	2	try
rare	scarce	3	answer
circular	round	4	sleepy
drowsy	sleepy	5	rough
moist	damp	6	buy
cease	stop	7	yearly
putrid	rotten	8	frightened
regret	sorrow	9	mad
portion	part	10	brave

Page 75 Words which save work

	A		B
1	widow	1	briefly
2	rescued	2	decide
3	died	3	correctly
4	returned	4	annually
5	homeless	5	suddenly
6	soon	6	miser
7	useless	7	bareheaded
8	mad; insane	8	capsized
9	disappeared		
10	improving		

Page 76 Twin words

	A		B	C
1	take	1	tongs	Own answers.
2	starts	2	key	
3	sure	3	head	
4	shoulders	4	wide	
5	out	5	foot	
6	sound	6	down	
7	lock	7	square	
8	fair	8	give	
9	hand	9	dogs	
10	hammer	10	safe	
11	cats			
12	far			

Page 77   Noises of creatures

A

donkeys; bray
lions; roar
sheep; bleat
cows; moo
dogs; bark
cockrels; crow
hens; cluck
pigs; grunt; squeal

B

1 wolves; howl
2 mice; squeak
3 geese; cackle; hiss
4 owls; hoot
5 snakes; hiss
6 bees; hum
7 rooks; caw
8 doves; coo
9 ducks; quack

C

1 cooing
2 squeaking
3 hooting
4 quacked
5 cawing
6 hissed
7 howling
8 humming
9 cackle
10 neighed; whinnied

Page 78   Rocky and the lioness

1   The lioness had come out of the scrub.
2   Rocky's heart thumped irregularly.
3   wicked; intelligent
4   The weapon was a rifle.
5   Rocky was fifty metres away from the lioness when it started to walk towards him.
6   Rocky was unable to see the chest of the lioness because its head was down.
7   Rocky aimed at a spot between the eyes of the lioness.
8   Rocky's bullet hit the ground behind the lioness.
9   The lioness growled, lashed its tail and charged.
10 The lioness was killed by Kukulu's spear.

Page 79   Sounds

A

1 train
2 saw
3 rain
4 steam
5 whistle
6 paper
7 bugle
8 hoofs
9 feet
10 gun

B

1 ticking
2 clatter
3 rustle
4 patter
5 lash; crack
6 howl
7 beat
8 singing
9 slamming
10 toot

C

1 shriek
2 call
3 patter
4 rumble
5 hiss
6 clatter
7 tramp
8 buzz

Page 80   Analogies

A

1 hive
5 cub

2 aunt
6 veal

3 narrow
7 fur

4 finger
8 hoof

B

florist		2	glove	3	elephant	4	wrist	
aeroplane		6	water, etc.	7	brewery	8	statue; sculpture	

Page 81   The doers of actions

A

climber
supplier
student
actor; actress
lodger
traveller
sailor
beggar
tourist
creator

B

1   cyclist
2   resident
3   decorator
4   inventor
5   warrior
6   manager
7   carrier
8   conquerors
9   inhabitant
10 kidnapper

Page 82   The correct order of sentences

A	B	C	D
3, 1, 2	5, 3, 2, 1, 4	3, 5, 1, 4, 2	2, 4, 5, 1, 3

Page 83   Abbreviations

A

Queen Elizabeth
page; pence
Before Christ
Department
Her Majesty
In the year of Our Lord
Post Office; Postal Order
Captain
Please turn over
ditto – the same
Royal Air Force
Her Majesty's Ship

B

1   Before Christ
2   Her Majesty's Ship
3   Captain
4   page
5   Department
6   Her Majesty
7   the year of Our Lord
8   Postal Order
9   Royal Air Force
10 ditto – the same

Page 84   Tom Sawyer and Aunt Polly

Aunt Polly seized Tom by his belt.
The mess on Tom's face and hands was jam.

3 Tom shouted, "My! Look behind you, Aunt!"
4 When Aunt Polly heard Tom's shout she whirled round and snatched her skirts out of danger.
5 Tom scrambled up the high board fence and disappeared over it.
6 When Aunt Polly had recovered from her surprise she broke into a gentle laugh.
7 Aunt Polly did not know what trick to look for because Tom's tricks were never the same.
8 Tom's punishment was to work on a Saturday.
9 Aunt Polly chose this punishment because Tom hated work and the other boys would be having a holiday.
10 This happened on a Friday.

Page 85   Rhymes

A
Winter

1	thrush	6	eat
2	bush	7	hedge
3	force	8	sedge
4	course	9	lurch
5	neat	10	perch

B
1 foul
2 meant
3 field
4 doubt
5 court
6 suite

C

1 wait
  await
  crate

2 despair
  declare
  swear

3 canteen
  machine
  scene

4 crane
  chain
  skein

5 fright
  height
  spite

Page 86   More fun with words

A
1 stage
2 beard
3 thorn
4 plums
5 slave
6 cloud
7 petals
8 march
9 stale

B
1 smash
2 plain
3 cream
4 fright
5 stole
6 paint
7 shoot
8 spoil
9 scent

Page 87　Proverbs

A
1　Waste not, **want** not.
2　Two **heads** are better than **one**.
3　Fine **feathers** make fine **birds**.
4　One good **turn** deserves **another**.
5　Cut your **coat** according to your **cloth**.

B
1　Fine feathers make fine birds.
2　Cut your coat according to your cloth.
3　Two heads are better than one.
4　Birds of a feather flock together.
5　One good turn deserves another.

Page 88　Similes

A
1　rock
2　peacock
3　church mouse
4　pancake
5　lightning
6　houses
7　feather
8　daisy
9　hills
10　fox

B
1　quick
2　flat
3　safe
4　fresh
5　old
6　steady
7　poor
8　cunning
9　proud
10　light

C
Pictures

as cunning as a fox
as light as a feather
as poor as a church mouse

as safe as houses
as old as the hills
as fresh as a daisy

D
1　pancake　　　2　hills　　　3　rock
4　church mouse　　5　lightning

Page 89　Variety in writing sentences

A
1　Last night the two boys went to see a film.
2　Up in the tall trees the rooks were cawing loudly.
3　Because he is so tall and strong my brother decided to become a policeman.
4　Owing to the very heavy rain the carnival was postponed.
5　Under a spreading chestnut tree the village smithy stands.

B
1 Michael emigrated to Canada soon after his father died.
2 A tramp was sheltering from the rain under the railway bridge.
3 Martin darted across the road without stopping to look if the road was clear.
4 The fireman jumped clear of the falling roof in the nick of time.
5 Roger failed his exam because he did not work.

C
Own answers.

Page 90   The golden fleece

1   Fifty heroes went aboard the Argo.
2   Orpheus liked playing the harp better than rowing.
3   At the first ringing note of the music the rowers felt the vessel move.
4   Pelias was standing on a promontory.
5   He wished he could blow out of his lungs the anger he was feeling, and so sink the galley with all on board.
6   The heroes made the time pass more pleasantly by talking about the Golden Fleece.
7   Helle fell into the sea and was drowned.
8   Phrixus was brought safely ashore by the faithful ram.
9   After the death of the ram its fleece was changed to gold.
10 The ram's fleece was kept hanging on a tree in a sacred grove.